Sport Lauderdale

Big Names and Big Games

Sport Lauderdale

Big Names and Big Games

A Sports Enthusiast's Guide to Broward County, Florida

Cynthia A. Thuma

The History Press

Published by The History Press
Charleston, SC 29403
www.historypress.net

Front cover: Brian Piccolo. *Courtesy of Wake Forest University Athletic Department.*
Back cover: *Courtesy of the Broward County Historical Commission, Edith Lewis Collection.*

First published 2007

Manufactured in the United States

ISBN 978.1.59629.145.4

Library of Congress Cataloging-in-Publication Data

Thuma, Cynthia.
Sport Lauderdale : a sports enthusiast's guide to big names and big games in Broward County, Florida / Cynthia A. Thuma.
p. cm.
Includes bibliographical references.
ISBN 978-1-59629-145-4 (alk. paper)
1. Sports--Florida--Broward County--History. 2. Athletics--Florida--Broward County--History. 3. Arenas--Florida--Broward County--History
I. Title.
GV584.F5T58 2007
796.09759'35--dc22
2007000649

Notice: The information in this book is true and complete to the best of our knowledge. It is offered without guarantee on the part of the author or The History Press. The author and The History Press disclaim all liability in connection with the use of this book.

Contents

Acknowledgements

Good beginnings are important. My beginning in sports came on an Oakland Park softball team called the Blue Jeans, led by two very enthusiastic and supportive coaches—Pat James and Lillian Pitcher. Their coaching, along with the support of my parents and brother, gave me a solid foundation and the desire to go as far as I could in sports. Along the way I was coached by excellent coaches such as Dr. Judy Blucker, who helped make sports an important part of my life. They still are.

Coaches are teachers of a rare and special variety, and I was fortunate to have been taught and coached by one of the nation's best—Dr. Billie Jo Jones, now retired from teaching and coaching at Florida State University. It is to Dr. Jones that this book is dedicated. Not only did Dr. Jones coach winning volleyball and softball teams for the Seminoles, she helped teach several generations of outstanding teachers and coaches. I am fortunate and grateful to have been one of her students, one of her athletes and a protégé.

Creation of a book of this type requires hundreds of hours of research and more importantly, the generous assistance of many people. They come from schools, professional sports teams and recreation departments. They are fellow journalists, sports administrators and folks from national sporting organizations. To them all, I offer my humble thanks: Craig Barnes, David Brousseau, Larry Bush, Louise Crocco, Gary Curreri, Saskia Fisher, Susan Gillis, Barbara Gonzalez, Barry Krauss, Rick Leffel, Rosie Leutzinger, Katrina McCormick, Chad Moller, Bill Plummer III, Jillian Printz, Jane Read, Sanya Richards, Sharon Robb, Lyn St. James,

Brita Schipner, George Smith, Diane Tomasik, Mark Tomasik, John Webb, David Winner, the sports information offices of Auburn University, Boston College, Broward Community College, College of the Sequoias, Florida Atlantic University, Lincoln Memorial University, University of Missouri, Nova Southeastern University and Wake Forest University. The following organizations also provided assistance: Amateur Softball Association of America, Professional Bowlers Association, the Spokane Shock, Old Dillard Art and Cultural Museum and the Miami Dolphins.

Dr. Ken Sargeant, a former high school football coach and administrator who also served as athletic director and football coach at Fort Lauderdale College, graciously shared memories of his forty years in Broward sports.

Finally, this book would never have come about without the assistance of the relentlessly generous and helpful staff of the Broward County Historical Commission: Christopher Eck, Helen Landers, Denyse Cunningham and Mary Rose Harding. They are a small group, but professional, enthusiastic, devoted to their cause and always a delight to work with.

INTRODUCTION

Location, location, location—that's supposedly the key to winning in business. It's also one of the keys to success in athletics, as Broward County, Florida, clearly demonstrates. Broward's location, its climate and the facilities it offers make it a natural training ground for winners in a variety of sports—including ice skating and hockey.

Not every superlative athlete to come from this area is profiled here, nor is every high school or youth league team to win state or national titles. The list would simply be too long. I'm sure some very worthy athletes are not profiled here, but this book has been created not as a definitive history, but rather as a sampler, a smattering of sports and athletes, which are hopefully representative of one of America's great sporting areas.

1

A Sense of Place

Broward County is packed with sporting venues from Miramar to Parkland. Many are used for local leagues and recreational play, but others, such as the BankAtlantic Center in Sunrise, are far more grandiose and used for professional sports. Here's a short tour:

Coral Springs

Coral Springs Aquatic Center: Opened in 1989, the center has played host to a variety of local, national and international swimming, diving, water polo and synchronized swimming competitions.

Coral Springs Tennis Center: Completed in 1993, the center was completed and quickly pressed into service as host site for the America's Red Clay Tennis Championships in 1993 and remained home to the tournament until 1998. Among the singles winners of the tournament were Jason Stoltenberg and Andrew Ilie.

Fort Lauderdale

International Swimming Hall of Fame and Aquatic Center: Noted architect Francis Abreu designed the Las Olas Beach Casino, at A1A and Southeast Fifth Street. The complex was the first Olympic-sized pool in the state and opened in 1926.

The casino pool was torn down in May 1966 and the International Swimming Hall of Fame and Aquatic Center, which had been constructed just west of the casino pool, opened in 1965. The complex underwent significant renovation and continues to be the site of many local, state, national and international meets.

The International Swimming Hall of Fame, located on the western edge of the property, is an archive and repository for swimming documents and memorabilia from all over the world as well as home to a swimming research center and an art gallery.

Lockhart Stadium and Fort Lauderdale Baseball Stadium: H.Y. "Doug" Lockhart Stadium was dedicated at halftime ceremonies of a Fort Lauderdale High–Central Catholic football game, September 18, 1959. Mayor John Russell, Monsignor John J. Looney and Edith Lockhart, widow of the former city commissioner, led the ceremonies. Central Catholic won the game, 6–0.

Hundreds of memorable high school football games, along with state football and soccer championship games have taken place at this municipal football and track stadium, but the facility grew to be so much more.

Lockhart Stadium served as home of the North American Soccer League's (NASL) Fort Lauderdale Strikers from 1977 until December 1983, when the Strikers left for Minnesota. The Minnesota Strikers avoided the demise of the NASL by joining the Major Indoor Soccer League, but folded anyway in 1988.

Save for a few special soccer games, Lockhart Stadium reverted to use as a football and track stadium. In 1998, however, soccer called again as the stadium became home to the Miami Fusion of Major League Soccer. About $5 million in renovations transformed the stadium from an all-purpose track/football/soccer facility to one more suitable for soccer alone. The Fusion operated from 1998 to 2001, and brought players such as Carlos Valderrama, Cle Kooiman and Preki. The team reached its heights under the coaching of former Fort Lauderdale Striker Ray Hudson, its final coach, who led the team to the Major League Soccer Supporters' Shield, for the league's best regular season record (16–5–5), although the season was curtailed because of the terrorist attacks on September 11, 2001. In early January of 2002, Major League Soccer announced its board of governors decided to terminate the Fusion and Tampa Bay Mutiny franchises.

The stadium's role as a soccer site cannot be diminished. The top teams in American soccer, along with World Cup teams and heralded pro

Florida Atlantic University Coach Howard Schnellenberger directs the Owls at a home game at Lockhart Stadium. *Florida Atlantic University Sports Information Office.*

teams from around the world such as the Boca Juniors of Brazil, Bayern Munich of Germany, Vasco de Gama of Brazil and the Glasgow Rangers of Scotland, have played at Lockhart.

In the 2003 season, the stadium underwent another transformation, becoming home to Florida Atlantic University's football program, led by legendary coach Howard Schnellenberger. The blue, yellow and white Fusion trim was stripped away, and on game days the east side of the stadium was festooned with red, white and navy and took on a festive air, with booths, games and entertainment.

The beginning of the end for Lockhart Stadium came on September 26 and the wee hours of September 27, 2006, when the Broward County Commission agreed to assist the Baltimore Orioles in a plan to revamp the Fort Lauderdale Stadium complex. The comprehensive plan included renovating the stadium, razing Lockhart Stadium and building a $38-million athletic complex that provides four athletic stadiums, four baseball diamonds and a main stadium to be used for football, soccer and other sports.

Fort Lauderdale Stadium, built just across Northwest Twelfth Avenue from Lockhart Stadium, opened in 1962 and served as the spring training home of the New York Yankees from that year until 1995, when the team departed for Legends Field in Tampa. Since 1901 the Yankees have trained in eighteen cities (among them Hamilton, Bermuda, in 1913), but no city served as the Bronx Bombers' home as long as Fort Lauderdale's thirty-three years. During that time, thousands of players came and went. Some reached the Major Leagues; most did not. One of the many players who advanced no further than Fort Lauderdale was Ron Williamson, subject of John Grisham's book *The Innocent Man: Murder and Injustice in a Small Town.* Williamson spent the entire 1977 season as a pitcher on the Fort Lauderdale Yankees' roster, his last stint as a professional player. He was convicted in 1988 of a 1982 murder in Oklahoma and was sentenced to death. Through the efforts of the Innocence Project, he was exonerated in April 1999. He died in December 2004.

In 1995, with the Yankees gone west, the Baltimore Orioles, who had made their spring home in St. Petersburg from 1992 to 1995, needed a home, and Fort Lauderdale's cozy 8,340-seat stadium was available.

In addition to spring training, the stadium has been used for minor league baseball, such as the Yankees' A-team—the Fort Lauderdale Yankees of the Florida State League, who played from 1962 to 1992 at the stadium. The Yankees were Florida State League champs in 1962, '64, '65, '80, '82 and '87.

The Fort Lauderdale Red Sox also played at Fort Lauderdale Stadium in 1993 as part of the Florida State League. Fort Lauderdale also had a team in the first incarnation of the Florida State League in 1919–1928: the Fort Lauderdale Tarpons, who played only in the ill-fated half-season of 1928.

Fort Lauderdale Stadium also was the site for filming of the 1983 film *Blue Skies Again,* about a female ballplayer, Paula Fradkin, who tries to break into the minor leagues with the Denver Devils, but finds the times

Fort Lauderdale Baseball Stadium, shown here in its early days, has been used for spring training, minor league baseball and high school championship games. *Broward County Historical Commission, Sun-Tattler collection.*

are not right for a woman to break into the male-dominated environment of baseball. The movie starred Harry Hamlin as team owner Sandy Mendenhall, Mimi Rogers as Liz West and Kenneth McMillan as Devils manager Dirk Miller. Also in the cast was a young actor who went on to bigger and better roles—Andy Garcia.

Beguiling as young Paula was Robyn Barto, who played softball at Fort Lauderdale High and was discovered while playing for Broward Community College at a college softball tournament in Miami. *New York Times* film critic Vincent Canby found Barto fresh and beguiling, more than he could say for the remainder of the cast.

"Except for Miss Barto, all the actors give performances that are as silly as their roles," he wrote.

HOLLYWOOD

Boggs Field: Named for city commissioner Lester Boggs, the park was the home of Fort Lauderdale College's men's baseball program for two seasons in the late 1970s. The college chose the Hollywood location because its athletic director, Ken Sargeant, had worked for Hollywood's recreation department.

"I got Fred Ferrara to coach," Sargeant said. "He was a Yankees' scout at the time. We played our games at Boggs Field and I got Ed Plaisted [longtime sports editor of the *Hollywood Sun-Tattler*] to umpire, so I knew the games would get in the paper."

The park now serves as home to the Hollywood Wildcats soccer program and the city's very successful Police Athletic League program.

Dowdy Field: Grocery store manager Earl Dowdy led an effort to build a baseball facility in Hollywood. The effort was embraced by city fathers and the city commission, and the field was built in 1933 alongside Dixie Highway and named in Dowdy's honor for his efforts in building support for the facility. It's a fair bet the Piggly Wiggly manager would have been proud to see how the field served the community.

In addition to use by city leagues and high school teams, the Baltimore Orioles used it for their spring training home for one year before the start of World War II and again in 1946 and 1947, when the ball club paid $500 each year to lease the park. After the pro players left, the diamond was pressed back into use in the summer by local baseball and softball teams. The baseball diamond at Dowdy Field still stands, but the field is mostly used for youth soccer these days.

The building in the southeast quadrant of the property originally had been an arena constructed by the Police Benevolent Association to provide a home for Wednesday night professional wrestling matches. The matches, which were wildly popular, provided revenue for the police to assist injured and ill officers. It also provided funds for the start of the city's very active Police Athletic League program, which now operates out of modern headquarters at Boggs Field.

Hard Rock Live: The 5,500-seat arena at the Seminole Hard Rock Hotel and Casino became home to the Florida Frenzy football team for the 2006 season. The Frenzy, a member of the National Indoor Football League, got its start as the Miami Morays in 2005, and moved north the next season. The Frenzy's drawing card was its general manager, former Miami Dolphins wide receiver Oronde Gadsden. The Frenzy went 12–17–0 and finished third in their division.

Pembroke Pines

Donnith H. Fletcher Veterans Memorial Park: This facility honors the memory of the first Pembroke Pines resident to become a casualty of the Vietnam War. It has become recognized as one of America's hotbeds of girls' softball. From eight-and-unders to eighteen-and-unders, Pembroke Pines teams have dominated on a national and international scale. A list of national and world championship teams is located in the softball section in the Sports of All Sorts chapter.

Pompano Beach

Municipal Stadium: The hole that Texas Rangers rookie outfielder Pete Incaviglia made with a line drive to the left-field fence during spring training of 1986 is gone now, but Municipal Stadium, damaged by Hurricane Wilma in 2005 and looking long in tooth, remains a home for baseball camps and amateur games. The stadium was dedicated on March 22, 1957, and the Washington Senators and the Texas Rangers used the cozy little stadium as their spring training home from 1961 to 1986. The Senators called it their spring training home from 1961 to 1971 and although the team was changed to the Texas Rangers and moved to Arlington in 1972, it kept its spring training home in Pompano Beach until 1986.

Municipal Stadium was host to two Florida State League programs: the Pompano Beach Mets (1969–73) and the Pompano Beach Cubs (1976–78).

The stadium enjoyed one last moment in the spotlight as the co-home (with Miami's Bobby Maduro Stadium) of the Gold Coast Suns of the short-lived Senior Professional Baseball Association in 1989–90. The Suns were one of the eight original franchises in the league for former Major League players and finished third in the league's Southern Division for the 1989–90 season. The Suns folded before the 1990–91 season; the league didn't make it to the midpoint of its second season, shutting down in December 1990.

The Suns were managed by Earl Weaver and boasted of a roster that included pitchers Joaquin Andujar, Stan Bahnsen and Luis Tiant. Field players included Bert Campaneris, Paul Blair, Cesar Cedeno, Rafael Landestoy and Rennie Stennett.

SUNRISE

BankAtlantic Center: Originally known as the Broward County Civic Arena, then the National Car Rental Center (1998–2002), Office Depot Center (2002–05) and currently the BankAtlantic Center, the $212-million indoor arena, located along the Sawgrass Expressway in southwestern quadrant of the county, became home to the Florida Panthers of the National Hockey League in 1998. The Panthers played their first years (1993–1997) at Miami Arena in downtown Miami, where the team's enthusiastic fans gained notice for tossing rubber rats on the ice after goals until the league banned the practice.

The arena also has played home to the Florida Bobcats of the Arena Football League from 1999–2001; when the team ceased operations, the Florida Pit Bulls of the American Basketball Association for 2005–2006 and was the host site of the ABA's 2005–06 All-Star Game. The Pit Bulls—who were coached by part-owner/player Tim Hardaway, a former Miami Heat great—announced that it would jump to the Continental Basketball League and become the Miami Majesty after the conclusion of the 2006 season. The team will begin play in Miami-Dade County in 2007.

The arena also was the host site for the Miami Jackals of Roller Hockey International, an inline hockey league, in 1999.

2

BASEBALL

Though baseball has never achieved the full-blown frenzy in Broward that it found in Miami-Dade and Palm Beach counties, Broward has shown itself over the long term as a fertile area for playing opportunities and player development. Baseball fans and players can find what they like on the diamonds throughout Broward County.

At the Major League level, Fort Lauderdale is one of the more delightful stops on the Grapefruit League circuit, having served for thirty-three years as the spring training home of the New York Yankees and since 1995, the home of the Baltimore Orioles.

Pompano Beach's Municipal Stadium hosted the Washington Senators from 1961 to 1971 and then the Texas Rangers from 1972 to 1986.

Hollywood's Dowdy Field was the spring training site of the Orioles one year before the start of World War II and in 1946 and 1947.

In 1991 Hollywood officials made a bid to lure the Montreal Expos south to their city when Montreal's lease with West Palm Beach ran out in 1995. The Hollywood group pointed out that nearly a quarter-million French Canadian tourists flock to their city each winter, but the Expos instead moved to Roger Dean Stadium in Jupiter, where they trained from 1998 to 2002.

Several Broward communities have had ties to minor league baseball. The Fort Lauderdale Yankees, a single-A team in the Florida State League, played from 1962 to 1992 at what was then called Fort Lauderdale Yankee Stadium. Fort Lauderdale also hosted a team in the FSL's first incarnation (1919–28) and was home to the Fort Lauderdale

Tarpons for the first half of the 1928 season. Pompano Beach also played host to two minor league programs: the Pompano Beach Mets (1969–73) and the Pompano Beach Cubs (1976–78). Deerfield Beach hosted the Sun Sox, a single-A affiliate of the Chicago White Sox, in 1966.

The Senior Professional Baseball Association started in Florida in 1989 by Jim Morley, who had played in the minors himself. The league was for players thirty-five and over (thirty-two and over for catchers) and attracted some easy-to-remember names from the game, including Vida Blue, Rollie Fingers and Luis Tiant.

Broward's tie to the league was through the Gold Coast Suns, who split their home games between Pompano Beach's Municipal Stadium and Bobby Maduro Stadium in Miami. The Suns were managed by legendary Orioles manager Earl Weaver and boasted of a roster that included pitchers Joaquin Andujar, Stan Bahnsen and Tiant. Field players included Bert Campaneris, Paul Blair, Cesar Cedeno, Rafael Landestoy and Rennie Stennett.

The St. Petersburg Pelicans triumphed in the league's only complete season (1989–90). The Suns finished third in the Southern Division and

Hoyt Wilhelm shows youths the fundamentals of pitching in a 1976 clinic at Fort Lauderdale Yankee Stadium. *Broward County Historical Commission, Sun-Tattler collection.*

Members of Fort Lauderdale's 1913 East Coast League champion team. Members included Herbert "Pops" Lewis, Roy Parrier, Frank Kraybill, Johnny Pellett, Carl Horton, John Windham, Joe Atkinson, Charles Berry, Charles G. Rodes Jr. and William J. "Cap" Reed. *Broward County Historical Commission.*

Above: Members of the Fort Lauderdale Tarpons, taken at Stranahan Field about 1921 to 1923. Members pictured included Herbert Lewis, Jasper Lawson, Art Hall, Charles Rodes, Jr., Charley Crim and H.S. "Shorty" Becker. The umpire is William J. Reed. *Broward County Historical Commission, Ruby Haberly Hamilton collection.*

Following pages: Members of Fort Lauderdale's 1915 town team. *Broward County Historical Commission, Edith Lewis collection.*

F.T.L

did not start the second season. The league only made it to the midpoint of the second season before collapsing.

Amateur baseball is very strong in Broward and has been from the start. Fort Lauderdale, like many Florida cities, sponsored a city team for the community's youth. Frank Stranahan donated land and money to get a baseball program rolling after the city's incorporation in 1913. The diamond was constructed later on the east side of the Fort Lauderdale High property at Broward Boulevard and Federal Highway. Stranahan later paid for fences and seats for the field, which also featured thatched chickee-style roofs over the dugouts. The team entered and won the East Coast League pennant in 1913 and in 1924. The East Coast League was, in essence, a minor league program, but much more loosely organized and supervised than today's minor leagues. Players came and went, and as playoff time approached, some of the arriving players were obviously ringers.

Two men named Les proved to be pivotal in Fort Lauderdale's early baseball years. Les McNeese was selected to play for the United States's 1936 Olympic demonstration baseball team. McNeese, along with Katy Rawls, represented Fort Lauderdale at Hitler's Berlin Olympics, and both did well, although the baseball demonstration wasn't what its promoters had hoped. The United States was supposed to have played a single demonstration game against Japan, but with tensions on the international scene roiling, the Japanese pulled out, leaving the promoters scrambling. In the end, they divided the U.S. squad into two teams. One team was called the U.S. Olympic team; the other was the World Champions team, for which McNeese played second base. On a lovely Berlin night in 1936, the teams played at Olympic Stadium in front of an appreciative audience of about 125,000, and McNeese's team pulled out a 6–5 victory.

The second Les was Les Sweetland (Lester Leo Sweetland), also known as "Sugar," a left-handed pitcher, who went on to play five years in the Majors. In 1927, at the age of twenty-six, Sweetland pitched his first game for the Philadelphia Phillies. He went 2–10 that year. His best year was 1929, when he went 13–11 and posted an ERA of 5.11. He spent four years with Philadelphia and one with the Chicago Cubs.

Other members of Fort Lauderdale's town team, later known as the Tarpons, were Orth Collins, who played five games for the New York Yankees in 1904 and five games for Washington in 1909. Collins died in Fort Lauderdale in 1949. Other players included Frank Tuppen, pitcher Charles Rodes, pitcher Douglas Brady, Charles Crim, Art Hall, Jasper Lawson and Joseph R. Moe. Managers included Charles Hoagland,

Pop Lewis, Karl Horton and William J. "Cap" Reed, who also served as umpire when he was not managing.

In 1921 members of the Fort Lauderdale team and the West Palm Beach Invincibles were arrested for playing baseball on a Sunday. In 1922 lawmen came visiting again, when Sheriff Paul Bryan strode onto the diamond at Stranahan Park during a game between Fort Lauderdale and Miami and ordered the arrest of Fort Lauderdale's entire team for a blue law violation. But the result was not the same as the previous year. A Miami judge was a player for the Miami team—whose members were not arrested—and assisted in defending the Fort Lauderdale team. A jury took ten minutes to deliberate before finding the Fort Lauderdale team not guilty.

College baseball is alive and strong through Broward Community College (BCC) and Nova Southeastern University's teams. The early direction of BCC's baseball program was under the direction of Leroy Wheat, a former Philadelphia Athletics pitcher. Wheat, who also was a professor of physical education at the college, was known to occasionally grant extra credit to students who could produce a copy of his baseball card.

Several members of the BCC baseball program went on to reach the Major Leagues. Among them were Don Newhouser, a graduate of Monsignor Pace High in Opa-Locka, who honed his pitching skills under Coach Wheat's guidance. Newhouser was drafted in the second round of the 1967 amateur draft by the Boston Red Sox and remained with the organization throughout his career. His Major League debut was June 15, 1972, and his final game was in 1974.

Craig Skok, all-county and all-conference player from Fort Lauderdale, went on to pitch at Florida State before being picked up as an undrafted free agent. His first Major League game was in 1973 for the Red Sox. He also pitched for the Texas Rangers before ending his career with the Atlanta Braves in 1979.

Fort Lauderdale College also fielded a team for a few years, playing out of Boggs Field in Hollywood.

For nearly thirty years, 1970 to 1997, the Big League World Series was held at Floyd Hull Stadium in southwestern Fort Lauderdale. The stadium was named to honor Hull, who served twenty-five years as president of the Fort Lauderdale Little League.

The Big League World Series was for players ages sixteen to eighteen and was generally dominated by teams from East Asia, whose fans stuffed the bleachers and chanted and cheered the entire game. The East Asian

Floyd Hull Stadium in 2006. The roof covering the bleachers was a victim of Hurricane Wilma, which did extensive damage to the complex. *Photo by Cynthia Thuma.*

teams' games were televised live in the wee hours to the teams' home countries. Still, Broward County's team—which, as the host, had a free pass into the tournament—fared well, winning in 1985 and 1992.

The tournament now makes its home in Easley, South Carolina, and in 2006 a team from South Broward won the South Regional championship and advanced to the World Series, the first visit by a Broward team since the program left in 1998.

Broward parks were the site of several early Khoury Baseball international championships at the Davie Sports Complex and Brian Piccolo Park.

The Pasadena Lakes section of Pembroke Pines won two Khoury national championships in the 1990s. The Juvenile Division Dodgers won the national IIB title in 1995, and the Atom Division Marlins won in 1996.

3

FOOTBALL

Broward County is indisputably one of the nation's hothouses for football talent. From peewee tackle teams to pro players, Broward builds gridiron winners. Glance at the players in the High School Heroes section of this book and you'll see the largest group of players represented there are football players.

Youth football is very strong in the Broward, Miami-Dade and Palm Beach county area, with players competing in a variety of programs. Leagues have come and gone over the years, and some of the smaller leagues have evolved into the two large leagues that serve Broward children. The American Youth Football League (AYFL) got its start in 1996, with six programs consisting of the remnants of the National Boys Football League. Teams joined slowly over the years and at the start of the 2006 season, there were fifteen programs in the league, fourteen of them from Broward County.

The Hollywood Optimist Football League (HOFL), which had teams in Palm Beach to Miami-Dade counties, evolved into the South Florida Youth Football League (SFYFL). After the 2005 season, another Broward league, the United Youth Football and Cheerleading League, which featured teams from Fort Lauderdale, Pompano Beach and Deerfield Beach disbanded, with the Northeast Rebels, Fort Lauderdale Jaguars and Deerfield Beach Raiders going to the AYFL and the Pompano Tigers and Pompano Eagles going to the SFYFL. At the start of the 2006 season, the SFYFL program had more than thirty participating programs in Broward, Miami-Dade and Palm Beach Counties.

Other programs have sampled one league and then moved to another, such as the Coral Springs Tackle Football Club. Coral Springs teams—

the Electras, Chargers and Dynamos—originally began play in the mid-1970s in the HOFL, but in 1998 moved to the AYFL.

High school football is where the stakes are ramped up. Broward schools have won ten state championships between 1964, when the Florida High School Activities Association began keeping records, and 2005. Leading the way is St. Thomas Aquinas, with three titles (Class 4A-1992, 5A-1997 and 4A-1999). Dillard has won twice (4A-1986 and 1989) and Chaminade-Madonna has as well (2A in 2003 and 2005). Hollywood Hills (4A-1973), the first Broward team to win a state championship, Ely (5A-2002) and Westminster Academy (1A-1990) each have won once.

The University of Miami, Florida Atlantic University and Florida International University have signed many Broward players to their rosters, and scouts from other colleges pay regular visits to Broward in the fall.

In 2003 Florida Atlantic University looked south from its home in Boca Raton to Lockhart Stadium for more than just players. The FAU Owls needed a home for their football program, which got its start in 2003 under the leadership of legendary coach Howard Schnellenberger, and it wasn't long until the Owls were flying high and playing in playoff games.

The Owls' first game at Lockhart Stadium wasn't particularly memorable. The Owls lost 45–17 to Valdosta State on September 6, 2003. A torrential rainstorm early in the game drove away most of the spectators and turned the field into a quagmire.

But Florida Atlantic wasn't the first college to call Lockhart Stadium home for its football program. That honor goes to the Seagulls of Fort Lauderdale College, who played out of Lockhart Stadium for two seasons in the late 1970s.

Drake College, a proprietary business college established in 1940, changed its name to Fort Lauderdale College in 1976. To stimulate enrollment, the school announced it would offer a football program under the guidance of its Canadian-born athletic director and football coach Ken Sargeant. Sargeant, who also was football coach at Nova High School, had approached Bill Markham, chair of Fort Lauderdale College's governing board, and convinced him an athletic program was what the school needed. Markham and his board accepted the proposal, hiring Sargeant as athletic director and football coach.

"We recruited sixty kids and set up a ten-game season," Sargeant said. "I set up the program, sold the ads. We even ran a carnival to raise money."

The Seagulls went 7–2–1 in their first season, losing only to Florida State's junior varsity and Mars Hill College. Among the victories were Fort Benning, Fort Bragg, St. Leo College (twice), Baptist Christian College and two games against junior varsity teams. The tie was a 30–30 deadlock against the University of Miami junior varsity. The victory over Fort Benning was particularly satisfying, Sargeant said.

"They wouldn't travel, so we had to go up to Georgia," he said. "They hadn't lost in two years and we went up and upset them, 13–2."

The Seagulls' first season was glorious, and topped off with two players named to the National Collegiate Football Association's All-America squad. The Seagulls were named the NCFA's Independent Conference Champion for 1978–79. The program played most of its home games at Lockhart Stadium, but not all.

"I remember we played a few at South Broward because I had gone to South Broward," Sargeant said. "We played a lot of games on the road, too." The Seagulls played a second season, then stored away their blue-and-gold jerseys forever.

Immediately before the start of the Fort Lauderdale College football program, and again in the late 1980s, Sargeant was at the forefront in an effort to bring football to Florida's community colleges. In the mid-'70s, Broward Community College and Miami-Dade Community College's North and South Campuses started tackle football clubs.

"We did it all in the spring. That was the concept," he said. "I had the team at BCC. We couldn't call the team the Seahorses, so we called them the Sharks. We used Nova's field and equipment, which was good because we were so close. We had two jamborees and then played two games." In those two games, Broward's unofficial squad beat Dade-North, 16–14, and Dade-South, 13–0.

In 1989 Sargeant and others took the matter to the community colleges. Backing the pro-football effort were former Miami Dolphins Manny Fernandez and Earl Morrall. The pro-football forces laid out their plans for the media at a press conference at the Old Heidelberg Restaurant in Hollywood.

Leading the anti-football forces was former Governor LeRoy Collins, architect of Florida's junior college system, who convinced the colleges the cost of adding football teams was too great. The proposal was rejected.

When the Miami Dolphins moved their training complex from St. Thomas University to the fan-friendly complex at Nova Southeastern University, Broward finally got a link to big-league football. The Dolphins'

Former Miami Dolphins tight end Jim Mertens is one of the players who remained in Broward after his playing years ended. Mertens worked in education and business in Broward and was active in coaching youth sports.

93,452-square-foot, $10-million training complex officially opened on July 11, 1993. In 2006 the team dedicated its 96,800-square-foot indoor training "bubble" that includes a regulation field, climate controls and lifelike artificial turf. The bubble was to have been dedicated on August 9, but inclement weather forced the squad inside on July 29.

Many Miami Dolphins players over the years have settled in Broward County, raised families and operated businesses and restaurants within the county, among them Dan Marino, Larry Ball, Jim Mertens, Daryl Porter, Jim Jensen, Mark Higgs, Dwight Stephenson and Autry Denson.

Football for women is big in Broward, too. Fort Lauderdale High won the first FHSAA flag football championship, beating Lake Worth, 14–7, for the title in 2003. Fort Lauderdale's Evette Young rushed for 161 yards and passed for 190 yards and five touchdowns to beat the Trojans. The Flying L's were runners-up to Apopka in the 2004 title game.

Also in 2004, the Florida Stingrays, a women's professional football team based in Dania Beach, lost, 53–12, to the Northern Ice in the Women's Professional Football League championship game in Kenosha, Wisconsin. Both teams were in their first year of play in the league. The Ice finished the season 12–0.

Though the Stingrays disbanded after the season, one player, linebacker Carol Clein, stayed in the game, becoming defensive line coach for Boyd Anderson High. Clein is one of three female scholastic football coaches in Florida in 2006.

Probably the first organized tackle football game for women in Broward was a benefit game for the Special Olympics, held at Coconut Creek High School in 1977. The teams played in uniforms and shoulder pads borrowed from Coral Springs and North Lauderdale's youth tackle programs.

4

Golf

Few places on earth are as lush and well suited to golf as Southern Florida. Historically, with acres and acres of undeveloped land, golf courses and golf course communities have been a nice fit in Broward County, and as of 2007 the county was home to more than seventy courses, varying from municipally owned Eco Golf Club in Hollywood, a nine-hole public course built on the site of a landfill, to high-end championship courses such as the Weston Hills Country Club in Weston and Plantation Preserve in Plantation. Many of South Florida's golf courses are part of housing developments, although many freestanding courses have been razed to provide acreage for commercial ventures.

Here's a tour of Broward's golf courses:

Adios Golf Course, Coconut Creek: Named for Adios (1940–1965), the champion Standardbred pacer that went on to sire nearly six hundred offspring, this 6,735-yard, par-72 course—designed by Arnold Palmer and Ed Seay and built in 1983—is better known as one of the very few golf courses nationwide (and one of two in Florida) that prohibits females. President George H.W. Bush played the course in 1992.

Arrowhead Golf Club, Davie: The course is 6,350 yards, par 70 and was designed by Bill Watts. The club was formerly owned by Miami Dolphins quarterback Earl Morrall. While Morrall was mayor of Davie, the clubhouse served as a sort of satellite city hall.

Bonaventure Country Club, Weston: The East and West Courses here are favorites for nonprofit tournaments, and the East Course has played host to the Dixie Amateur. The East Course, designed by Joe Lee and opened in 1972, is a par-72 layout that measures 7,001 yards; the West Course, designed by Charles Mahannah and opened in 1972, is 6,128 yards and par 70. The complex's signature hole is number three on the East Course, a formidable and picturesque waterfall hole.

Carolina Club, Margate: Designed by Bruce Devlin and Robert von Hagge and opened in 1989, Carolina Club is a 6,550-yard, par-72 layout.

Colony West Country Club, Tamarac: Colony West's Championship Course has always been a handful. Designed by Robert von Hagge and Bruce Devlin and built in 1971, the course originally was a monster 7,553-yard, par-72 layout. In 1981 it was shortened to par 70, 6,648 yards. In 1985, with a change of ownership, it was lengthened again to par 71, 7,312 yards. Colony West has the longest par-71 course in Florida. The Glades Course, which opened in 1972, is a far more sedate 4,207 yards and par 65.

Continental Golf and Tennis Club, Coral Springs: Originally opened as Broken Woods Country Club.

Cooper Colony Golf and Country Club, Cooper City: A fixture of the bedroom community almost from its start, the 3,820-yard, par-60 Executive Course was designed by Pat Pattison and opened in 1959.

Coral Ridge Country Club, Fort Lauderdale: A historic course in this golf-crazy area, made more by its ties to the Jones family. Robert Trent Jones Sr. designed the course, oversaw its construction and opened it in 1954. The 7,095-yard, par-72 layout was built over the soft, flat terrain, requiring Jones to build up the land and dig lakes to make it intriguing. The club is the host site of the Doherty/Jones Challenge Cup, an international championship for amateur women golfers, and one of the events of the Orange Blossom Tour, held each January.

Robert Trent Jones Sr. died in June 2000, about a year after suffering a stroke. The Coral Ridge Country Club property, along with that of neighboring American Golfers Club was acquired from Jones's sons Rees and Robert Trent Jr. in 2004 by a group of well-connected investors who planned to significantly upgrade the Coral Ridge course and to build upscale homes on the abandoned American Golfers property.

Country Club of Coral Springs, Coral Springs: A 6,779-yard, par-72 private equity course designed by Edmund Ault and opened in 1969. This course served as host of the 1971 Coral Springs Open stop on the PGA Tour. Lee Trevino won the event after prevailing in an eighteen-hole playoff with Jack Nicklaus.

The clubhouse of Eco Golf Club, which bills itself as the most beautiful nine-hole golf course in Florida. *Photo by Cynthia Thuma.*

Crystal Lake Golf Club, Pompano Beach: This course was redesigned by Rees Jones in 1981.

Deer Creek Golf Club, Deerfield Beach: Designed by Arthur Hills and opened in February 1971, Deer Creek, a par-72, 7,050-yard course, was renovated in 2004. The club hosted the LPGA Whirlpool Championships of Deer Creek from 1980 to 1982, a tournament that later became the Mazda Classic from 1983 until the tournament moved to Stonebridge Golf and Country Club in Boca Raton in 1986.

Tournament winners included Hollis Stacy (twice), Joanne Carner, Sandra Palmer (twice), Pat Bradley and Sylvia Bertolaccini. The course also has served as home for the 2002 United States Golf Association Amateur and the 2003 Senior Open.

Deerfield Country Club, Deerfield Beach: An eighteen-hole, par-63 private course, designed by William Follet Mitchell and opened in 1964.

Diplomat Country Club and Spa, Hallandale: Designed by Red Lawrence and opened in 1957.

Eagle Woods Golf and Country Club, Miramar: An eighteen-hole, semi-private course built in 1974. The course measures 6,650 yards and plays at par 72.

Eco Golf Club, Hollywood: A lovely, well-maintained nine-hole municipal course built over a landfill, it is 2,265 yards, par 32 and opened in 1982.

The Club at Emerald Hills, Hollywood: Designed by Bruce Devlin and Robert von Hagge and built in 1969, the club is currently a par 72, 7,280 yards off the back tees. The course was redesigned in 1989, reconstructed in 1999 and its greens were renovated in 2000. The club has hosted qualifiers for the Honda Classic, Doral and the U.S. Amateur. Larry Ziegler was named the club's touring pro in 1981.

Flamingo Lakes Country Club, Pembroke Pines: An eighteen-hole course built in 1984.

Fort Lauderdale Country Club, Plantation: Originally opened as Fort Lauderdale's Westside Golf Club, the south course was opened for play in December 1926. The clubhouse was designed by Francis Luis Abreu. The north course opened for play in 1951 and renovated in 1999. The course now operates as a private equity club.

Grande Oaks Country Club, Davie: Built in 1961 by William Follet Mitchell and opened as Rolling Hills Golf Course. In 1979 and early 1980, nine holes of the course were used as the site for "Bushwood Country Club" in the 1980 film *Caddyshack*, starring Bill Murray, Chevy Chase and Rodney Dangerfield. The course was selected because filming was done during the winter months and the film was supposedly set in the Midwest. The course looked Midwestern and had no palm trees. For years afterward, Bushwood Country Club sweatshirts and caps were on sale in the pro shop. In 1996 the course was purchased by H. Wayne Huizenga, renovated and redesigned by Raymond Floyd. The private equity club is now 6,905 yards.

Grand Palms Resort, Pembroke Pines: Grand Palms offers golfers an uncommon option, with three nine-hole courses, so players can pick the course with the degree of difficulty to best suit their game or tastes. Designed by Wade Northrup and built in 1986.

Hillcrest Golf and Country Club, Hollywood: Home to two courses—the par-72 championship layout at 6,516 yards, and the par-54 executive course, at 1,599 yards.

Hollybrook Golf Club, Pembroke Pines: A semi-private pair of courses. The championship is an eighteen-hole layout, 6,398 yards designed by Robert von Hagge and built in 1966. The nine-hole executive course is 2,155 yards, par 36.

Hillsboro Pines Golf, Deerfield Beach: Located within the sprawling Century Village complex, this semi-private course designed by Joe Lee opened in 1975. Its eighteen holes measure 3,699 yards, par 68.

Hollywood Beach Golf Resort, Hollywood: Designed in 1924 by legendary golf course designer Donald Ross (1872–1948).

Hollywood Beach Country Club and Golf Resort, Hollywood: Designed by H.C. Tippets in 1925. Redesigned by Charles Mahannah in 1955.

Inverrary Country Club, Lauderhill: All three courses were designed by respected course designer Robert Trent Jones Sr. The East Course, which opened in 1970, has served as host to PGA and LPGA tournaments. The Jackie Gleason Inverrary Classic (which later became the Honda Classic) started there in 1972 and stayed until 1983. Jack Nicklaus won the Tournament Players Championship there in 1976, and the LPGA Phar-Mor at Inverrary was held there in 1990 and 1991. Be sure and check out the plaque marking the spot at the fifth hole (then the fourteenth) where Jack Nicklaus knocked in a birdie from to win the Gleason tournament by one stroke in 1978. The course, which has undergone significant renovation from its new owners over the past few years, is 7,112 yards, par 72, from the championship tees. The West Course was opened in 1971 and is a par-71, 6,621-yard layout. The Executive Course is par-61, 3,314 yards and was opened in 1970.

Jacaranda Golf Club, Plantation: Both courses were designed by Mark Mahannah. The East Course, which opened in 1971, was redesigned by Bobby Weed in 2005. The course has hosted mini-tour events, qualifying site of the PGA Tour, Florida Open and U.S. Amateur. The West Course was opened in 1972 and also has been redesigned by Bobby Weed.

Lago Mar Country Club, Plantation: A scenic par-72, 6,691-yard course in western Plantation.

Lauderhill Golf Course, Lauderhill: A nine-hole municipal course, par 30, opened in 1975. The course was named a First Tee site in March 2002.

Leisureville Fairway, Pompano Beach: A cozy nine-hole layout that opened in 1969, Leisureville Fairway is 745 yards, par 27.

Margate Executive Golf Course, Margate: A nine-hole course designed by Bill Dietsch and opened in 1982. The course measures 1,512 yards, par 30.

Oak Tree Country Club, Fort Lauderdale: A private eighteen-hole, par-71 course.

Orangebrook Country Club, Hollywood: The two historic municipal courses are a hub of golf activity in Hollywood. The tougher East Course is par 72 and 6,563 yards with lots of water. The West Course is longer, at 6,626 yards, par 71. Property for the courses was purchased by the city of

Hollywood in June 1934. On July 31 of that year, an ordinance was passed authorizing creation of a municipal golf course with the stipulation that cost of construction and maintenance would not be borne by the city. A commission was formed, headed by citrus grower Floyd Wray, to develop the land into the golf course. A.J. Ewing supervised creation of the first nine holes that were developed. Three days after the ordinance's passage, the commission was hard at work. Wray offered to loan the city $250,000 to clear the land and get construction started. The city approved the offer. A membership drive (with individual memberships selling at $35 each) began as a way of providing operating capital; even snowbirds were offered memberships. Blocks of daily play tickets (at $1 per round) were sold to hotels, travel agencies, tour operators and merchants.

The commission recognized quickly that there were a few things going in their favor. One was that the golf course site has been the site of an earlier nine-hole course, laid out in 1926. About $15,000 in labor had been completed on the course, and six of the nine holes were practically complete, but work had been abandoned after the 1926 hurricane.

Another promising feature of the property was its orange grove. The commission was authorized to sell the orange crop with profits going

A young golfer gives his four-iron a workout at Orangebrook's driving range. *Photo by Cynthia Thuma.*

toward the course construction. The first year's harvest was projected at 750 boxes, bringing in $500, but sales didn't meet projections because a significant amount of the oranges were stolen. Farmers still were working the eastern portion of the property, where the second nine holes were to be located. They were permitted to remain until their crops were harvested in early spring of 1935.

Funding was a problem throughout development and construction of the course. Commission members tried a variety of ideas to raise money and the commission was authorized to borrow money from the city and its citizens.

The first nine holes of the East Course were opened on February 1, 1935, and by that time Ewing had left the project. Ralph Young, a friend of city founder Joseph Young, the original architect of the course and the person who selected the site for the course, was hired to lay out the remainder of the course, which opened July 1, 1936. The East Course served as host to the 1938 Hollywood Open, which was won by Byron Nelson and drew the sport's superstars of the day, including Sam Snead and Ben Hogan.

Each January, Orangebrook hosts the Women's International Four-Ball Tournament, an event of the Orange Blossom Tour for top women amateurs. Among the golfers to have played in the four-ball event are Babe Zaharias, Louise Suggs, Leslie Shannon, Patty Berg, Peggy Kirk Bell and Michelle McGann.

Oriole Golf and Tennis Club, Margate: Designed by Bill Dietsch and opened in 1982, the par-72 course measures 6,418 yards.

Palm-Aire Country Club, Pompano Beach: Palm-Aire is Broward's big daddy of golf with five courses, four of them at championship length. The best known of the courses is the Mighty Oaks, designed by Tom and George Fazio and built in 1971. The course was redesigned by Fazio Design, Inc., in 1998. Mighty Oaks is a par-72 course, 6,747 yards off the championship tees and has hosted the Florida Open, Nike South Florida Classic and Dixie Amateur.

The oldest of the courses is the Pines, designed in 1968 by Robert von Hagge and Bruce Devlin. The layout is 6,610 yards, par 72, and the course has played host to the Florida Open and Broward Amateur Tournaments. The Palms course was designed by William Mitchell in 1972 and was renovated in 1996 by Karl Litten and Lorie Viola. The course is 6,931 yards, par 72.

Also designed in 1972 was the Cypress Course, at 6,868 yards, par 72, designed by Tom and George Fazio. The course had hosted Florida Open and Dixie Amateur. The Sabals course, designed in 1969 by von Hagge and Devlin, is a par-58, 3,395-yard layout.

Parkland Golf Club, Parkland: A dramatic, lovely 7,118-yard, par-72 private equity course designed by Greg Norman and opened in 2004.

Pembroke Lakes Golf Club, Pembroke Pines: Designed by Howard and John Watson and opened in 1974, Pembroke Lakes is a par-72 course measuring 6,555 yards. In the waning days of December 2006, the Pembroke Pines city commission voted to pay for $7 million worth of renovation and upgrades to their municipal course.

Pine Island Ridge Country Club, Fort Lauderdale: An eighteen-hole layout covering 4,886 yards, par 64. The course opened in 1976.

Pines Par 3 Golf Course, Hollywood: A hang-loose atmosphere pervades this friendly par 3. The course was designed by Miles Wadkins and opened in 1964.

Plantation Preserve Country Club, Plantation: This lovely par-72 municipal course just over 7,100 yards was designed by the firm of von Hagge, Smelek and Baril and opened in 2005.

Pompano Beach Golf Course, Pompano Beach: This features two courses, Pines and Palms. The LPGA Pompano Beach Classic was played there on February 16–18, 1973. Sandra Palmer won the tournament; Betty Burfeindt finished second.

Springtree Golf Course, Sunrise: Located in a community originally incorporated as the Sunrise Golf Village, Springtree Golf Club is an eighteen-hole, par-61 layout at 4,198 yards, designed by Bill Dietsch and opened in 1972.

St. Regis Golf Club, Fort Lauderdale: This course was designed by Dick Wilson and opened in 1969.

Sunrise Country Club, Sunrise: A privately owned course open to the public. Designed by Bill Watts Jr., the course is eighteen holes, par 72, 6,668 yards, opened in 1950.

Sunset Lakes Phase III, Sunrise: A private nine-hole par-31 executive course opened in 1981.

Sunset Lakes Phase IV, Sunrise: A private nine-hole course opened in 1981.

Sunset Golf Club, Hollywood: A nine-hole course designed for owner Henry Cieri by Robert S. "Red" Lawrence. The cozy clubhouse was designed by Kenneth Spry and the course was opened in 1952. Sunset became the hub of Hollywood's golf activity under the ownership of pro golfer Bobby Goodman, who was honored posthumously by the PGA of America with its Lifetime Achievement Award. Goodman, of Plantation, was inducted into the South Florida PGA in 2002. A $2,500 scholarship bearing Goodman's name is awarded annually to a high school senior or college underclassman living in Florida whose parents are employed in or retired from the golf industry. Nick Boros is the course's current professional.

Tam O'Shanter Golf Club, Pompano Beach: Designed by Pat Pattison in 1964 and redesigned by Rees Jones in 1981.

Tournament Players Club at Eagle Trace, Coral Springs: The 7,040-yard, par-72 course was designed by Arthur Hills and opened in 1983. Eagle Trace served as home to the PGA's Honda Classic for nine years—1984 to 1991, and again in 1996.

Tournament Players Club at Heron Bay, Coral Springs: A par-72, 7,268-yard course designed by Mark McCumber and opened in 1996. Heron Bay served as home to the PGA's Honda Classic from 1997 to 2002, and is a daily fee course named by *Golf* magazine as one of the "Top Ten Places You Can Play."

Weston Hills Country Club, Weston: A pair of long, beautiful courses designed by Robert Trent Jones Jr. on the western edge of the county. The Tour Course at 7,069 yards, opened in 1990 and served as home to the Honda Classic from 1992 to 1995, the Dan Marino Celebrity Invitational from 1992 to 2001 and the LPGA Chrysler-Plymouth Tournament of Champions in 1997. The Players course, at 7,272 yards, opened in 1995.

Woodlands Country Club, Tamarac: Two superbly maintained private courses, both par 72, designed by the Devlin-von Hagge team and built in 1969. The East Course measures 6,722 yards and the West Course measures 6,825 yards.

Woodmont Country Club, Tamarac: Two private courses designed by Brucc Devlin and opened in 1974. The Cypress Course is 7,043 yards; the Pines Course is 6,283.

Wyndmoor Community Golf Club, Coconut Creek: A par-60 course measuring 3,456 yards, Wyndmoor opened in 1974.

Gone But Not Forgotten

American Golfers Club, Fort Lauderdale: A popular 3,002-yard, par-58 course with driving range designed by Robert Trent Jones Sr., in 1958 and located on Federal Highway at the intersection with Northeast Thirty-eighth Street.

Bogey's Driving Range and Par 3, Davie: The clubhouse still stands, but the course was razed for development.

Lauderdale Lakes Country Club and Golf Motor Lodge, Lauderdale Lakes. An eighteen-hole executive course located at the southeast corner of 441 and Oakland Park Boulevard, razed to build a shopping center. In 1963 a round cost $1.75 during prime time or $1.25 after 3:00 p.m.

Monterey Golf Course, Tamarac: Originally opened in 1968 as The Mainlands Club.

Palm Lakes Golf Course, Margate: Lodged between a pair of condominiums on Atlantic Boulevard, Palm Lakes was a delightful little executive course built alongside a pair of small lakes.

Palumbo's Golf Course, Hollywood: Created as a golf course for blacks in the days of segregation, Palumbo's was situated along Stirling Road and opened in 1953.

Pompano Park Par 3, Pompano Beach: Created by Frederick van Lennep as an addition to the Pompano Park harness racing complex, a pleasant, sandy course dotted with short-leaf slash pines. It was the first golf course in the nation to be located on the grounds of a harness racing park. The course was razed for commercial use.

Raintree Golf Resort, Pembroke Pines: Designed by Charles and Mark Mahannah in 1984, the course is par-72, 6,456 yards, but is set to close in mid-2007 to become a housing development.

Richardson Golf Course, Wilton Manors: George Richardson, a native of Ireland who built golf courses for some of the best golf course architects in the United States—Donald Ross and Albert Warren Tillinghast—came south in the 1920s to build courses in Florida. He worked for Francis Abreu building what is now the south course at Fort Lauderdale Country Club. He moved on to Montauk, New York to build a course for Miami Beach developer Carl Fisher, but never forgot Broward County. In 1936 Richardson was ready to retire and decided to build his own course to run. The result was the 2,820-yard, par-34, nine-hole layout located on Wilton Drive at the entrance to the city. The Richardson family established their home on the eastern edge of the property and lived there long after the course was razed to build condominiums.

Sabal Palm Golf Club, Tamarac: A relatively flat course with minimal bunkers, trees and just a touch of water here and there, Sabal Palm was a favorite of older golfers and those who had mobility problems, but still loved the game

South Side Golf Course, Fort Lauderdale: The course was plowed over for construction of Fort Lauderdale's airport in 1929.

Broward County has served as home for a large number of accomplished golfers.

Don E. Beattie Jr. went on to play golf at Broward Community College and Georgia Southern, then became a PGA pro, but most enjoyed the teaching and administrative aspects of the sport. He returned home to Pompano Beach to become an assistant pro at Pompano Beach's municipal golf course, then moved on to become director of golf at the Polo Club in Boca Raton from 1985 to 1993. His next stop was the Medallion Club, in Columbus, Ohio, where he worked from 1993 to 1996. He returned to Florida in 1996 to become director of golf at Addison Reserve, in western Delray Beach, then signed on as director of golf at Mirasol, in Palm Beach Gardens from the club's opening in 2001 until his death in 2006.

Julius Boros gave up a career as an accountant at thirty to play the PGA Tour. He ended up winning eighteen career titles, including U.S. Open crowns in 1952 and 1963 and a PGA Championship in 1968. His personality endeared him to many fans and he became one of the game's well-loved figures. His son Guy also played professionally.

Boros suffered a heart attack and died at Coral Ridge Country Club in May 1994. He was posthumously named to the South Florida PGA Hall of Fame in 2005.

Julia Boros-Petit is Julius Boros's granddaughter. Named a Junior All-America by the American Junior Golf Association, Boros graduated thirteenth in her class of 333 at St. Thomas Aquinas High School and went on to the University of Georgia, where she won the Edith Munson Award as the Senior All-America golfer with the best grade-point average. Boros-Petit went on to play on the Futures Tour and in LPGA events.

Donna Cusano-Wilkins played some of her best golf at the University of Miami, where she won the Southern Methodist University Roundup and Florida State Intercollegiate Championship, both in 1984, the year the Hurricanes won the NCAA national championship.

At age twelve, *Mike Donald* turned his back on baseball to be the best he could be in golf, thanks to the gift of a set of clubs from his parents, Bill and Pearl. He went on to win the 1973 Florida Junior championship and headed off to Broward Community College, where he medaled to lead the Seahorses to the 1974 National Junior College Athletic Association title, becoming a two-time NJCAA All-America along the way. He then received a Chris Schenkel scholarship to Georgia Southern University. He turned pro in 1978 and joined the PGA Tour in 1980, playing on it for more than a quarter century. Donald won the 1989 Anheuser-Busch Classic and tied the Masters's rookie record for low first-round score with 64 in 1990. He shot thirty-one on the first nine holes, tying Mark Lye's 1984 record. His first-round score of 64 tied Lloyd Mangrum's first-round rookie score set in 1940. But the fire didn't last long. Donald followed with an 82, then settled in for rounds of 77 and 76 for a 299 total, finishing forty-seventh and earning a check for $3,900.

Later in the year he was runner-up to Hale Irwin in the 1990 U.S. Open that went into a nerve-wracking nineteen-hole playoff. Other victories included the 1984 JC Penney Classic with Vicki Alvarez, and the 1990 Sazale Classic with his close friend Fred Couples.

Cindy Hill was a Michigander who went to the University of Miami. She played as an amateur through age thirty-one then played on the LPGA Tour out of Fort Lauderdale. She joined the LPGA in 1979 and won the 1984 Rail Charity Classic and the 1987 S&H Green Stamp Classic.

Barbara Mizrahie was born and raised in Indonesia. After moving to the United States, she settled in Fort Lauderdale and played out of Inverrary Country Club in Lauderhill.

Leslie Pearson, of Fort Lauderdale, didn't start playing golf until age twenty-four and only competed as an amateur for a year before turning pro in October 1985.

Patti Rizzo was born in Hollywood in 1960 and lived there through age twelve. Basketball was her sport of choice until she suffered a broken ankle, and on the advice of her family doctor, took up golf. She played her first rounds while still in a cast. She attended and played for the University of Miami and was the top-ranked amateur in the United States in 1980, the year she also won the Mexican Amateur.

Rizzo joined the LPGA Tour in 1982, where she was named the Rookie of the Year and finished in the top ten in five tournaments that year. Her first pro victory was the 1983 Boston Five Championship. She also won the Corning Classic (1985), Sara Lee Classic (1988), Red Robin Kyocera Inamori Classic (1989) and in that year also teamed with Mike Hill to win the Seniors Mazda Classic, worth $250,000 each.

She retired from the LPGA Tour in 2000 and now coaches Barry University's women's golf team. She lives in her hometown of Hollywood again with husband, Jacques Depardon, and their two children, occasionally playing events on the LPGA and Legends tours.

Sue Smith, a native of Fort Lauderdale, was a Broward Community College student who was the National Junior College Athletic Association national runner-up in 1982 and its champion in 1983. She went on to a year at Florida Atlantic then onto the LPGA Tour, where she was dogged by injuries.

5

Sports of All Sorts

Auto Racing

The heart of auto racing in Broward County formerly beat at the Hollywood Speedway, a drag strip also known as Miami-Hollywood Motorsports Park and by several other names.

There were other racing sites scattered around Broward, though, most of them short-lived, such as Davie Drags on the old Forman Field property, now occupied by Nova Southeastern University. Other racetracks were in Pompano Beach and Hollywood.

The Hollywood Speedway opened in March of 1966 and the top names in drag racing, among them Don "Big Daddy" Garlits and Shirley "Cha Cha" Muldowney, raced there.

The track was located next to the Hollywood Sportatorium and was razed in December 1992 for construction of the Silver Lakes development.

One of NASCAR's pioneers was *Benny Georgeson*, of Fort Lauderdale, who competed in NASCAR's first season in 1949. Georgeson drove his Buick to the first Strictly Stock championship five laps around the Broward Speedway's two-mile paved track.

Lyn St. James, who lived in Plantation from 1970 to 1979 and in Fort Lauderdale from 1979 to 1992, got her racing career off the starting line while living in Broward County. "I started racing in 1974 in the Sports Car Club of American and was a member of the Florida region where I won regional championships and placed on a national level until 1979," she said. "I raced in the 12 Hours of Sebring and 24 Hours of Daytona in the IMSA Camel GT Series, where I was part of the winning teams in the 1980s and 1990s. I also raced in the Miami Grand Prix in the early 1980s and the SCCA Tran Am Series in West Palm Beach." St. James moved to Ormond Beach and now lives in Indianapolis.

Lynn St. James during her years in Broward County. *LSJ Motorsports.*

A contemporary of St. James is *Mishael Abbott*, of Coral Springs, who got her start in karting, then advanced to the Sports Car Club of America, Star Mazda Series and the Indy Pro Series. Her goal is to be the first woman to win the Indianapolis 500.

Former Top Fuel dragster *Darrell Gwynn*, a Miami native, moved to Broward after his near-fatal accident in 1990 at Santa Pod Raceway in England. He and his family live in Weston and his foundation's headquarters are in Davie.

Basketball

The joke goes that in South Florida basketball is the way athletes keep in shape between football and baseball seasons. That's a bit of a stretch, of course, but many South Florida athletes do prefer sports that allow them to enjoy the fresh air and healthful climate. Basketball still has its charms, though, whether played indoors in a gymnasium or outdoors in the fresh air. Broward County offers plenty of opportunities from the youth level through college play and adult leagues.

In 1997 the Florida Youth Basketball Association got its start with ten teams and has grown to more than seventy-five. The league includes elite programs from Miami-Dade, Broward, Palm Beach, Martin and St. Lucie Counties. Broward County also is host to Upward programs, city- and county-based programs, YMCA programs and more.

Among high school girls, Broward County teams have won twenty-three state championships between 1976 and 2005. They include Coral Springs, Deerfield Beach, Dillard, Ely, Fort Lauderdale, Hallandale, Plantation, South Broward, Taravella and Westminster Academy. Among the eighteen boys' teams that have won state championships between 1922 and 2005 are teams from Boyd Anderson, Deerfield Beach, Dillard, Ely, Hallandale, Hollywood Christian, Pompano Beach, St. Thomas Aquinas and Westminster Academy.

The Kruel Classic, which was started in 1990, gives thirty-two of the nation's top prep teams (sixteen boys' teams and sixteen girls' teams) the chance to play in a holiday tournament in paradise. The tournament was named to honor James P. Kruel, of Coral Springs, who died of a heart attack at forty-one while playing basketball in a men's league game in Coral Springs. Kruel, the father of five children, was well known and loved in the community for his work coaching and teaching youth, including his own

Hallandale High coach Greg Samuel, center, prepares to whoop it up as the Chargers win the 1987 Class 3A title 80–71 over Orlando Jones. Samuel was a standout at Broward Community College and Florida State University during his college career. *Broward County Historical Commission, Sun-Tattler collection.*

basketball-loving children. The Kruel Classic has grown to become the nation's largest and most prestigious prep basketball tournament.

The National Car Rental Center in Sunrise served as home to the Florida Pit Bulls of the American Basketball Association for 2005–06 and also served as host site of the ABA's 2005–06 All-Star Game. The Pit Bulls were coached by part-owner and player Tim Hardaway, a former Miami Heat player. The Pit Bulls jumped to the Continental Basketball League in 2006 and became the Miami Majesty.

A few professional players have come from Broward County, among them Mitch Richmond, Keyon Dooling and Clarence Gilbert.

BEACH VOLLEYBALL

The Association of Volleyball Professionals, the ruling body for professional beach volleyball, brought its first tournament to Florida shores in 1982, to Clearwater Beach. By 1990 the AVP had found its way to the East Coast, with the $60,000 Miller Lite Open on the beach near the Yankee Clipper Hotel. Karch Kiraly and Kent Steffes won the tournament and opened the doors for the sport. A variety of beach volleyball tours crisscross South Florida's beaches now, offering competition for amateur and professional male and female players.

BOWLING

Broward County twice hosted Professional Bowlers Association tour events—the 1976 Dick Weber Five-Star Open at Don Carter's Tamarac Lanes, a $14,000 payday for winner Earl Anthony, and the 1991 Bud Light Classic at Don Carter's Sawgrass Lanes, won by Bob Benoit.

Broward has developed a few good bowlers over the years, but none approach the consistency of Bob Handley, who seemed to always finish in the money. Handley played out of Pompano Beach for many years (he makes his home in Winter Park now).

Handley's Professional Bowlers Association victories started in 1981 in Alameda, California; the 1982 Greater Miami Sunshine Open; 1983 Houston Open; 1987 Greater Hartford Open; 1990 Columbia 300 Open in Austin, Texas. He also has one Senior Tour title, the 2003 Senior Northwest Classic in Beaverton, Oregon.

Above: Bob Handley. *Professional Bowlers Association.*

Right: Sal Bongiorno. *Professional Bowlers Association.*

Other bowlers of note from Broward:

Sal Bongiorno, Hollywood: At the PBA's Portland tournament in 1975, Bongiorno finished first after forty-two games, but lost in the championship.

Storm DeVincent, Tamarac: DeVincent won $25,000 in July 2004 for winning the top spot in the Match Play Shootout finals in Las Vegas and finished fourth in the Fair Lanes National Resident Professional Championship in Orlando.

Butch Gearhart, Fort Lauderdale: Won the 1969 Newark Kiwanis Open. He later moved to Houston.

Rich Sajak, Coral Springs: Cashed a $27,000 check as winner of the 1984 Miller High Life Open in Milwaukee.

Lou Scalia, Hollywood: Won the 1967 ABC Masters Championship.

BOXING

Broward County is home to numerous boxing venues, such as the War Memorial Auditorium, Diplomat Hotel and the former Sunrise Musical Theater, among them.

Broward also was home to several well-known boxers. *Trevor Berbick*, found murdered in a Jamaican church courtyard in 2006, lived in Miramar during his boxing years.

Rocky Marciano, who compiled a 49–0 record during his career in the ring, retired in April of 1956, at thirty-three to a waterfront home in Fort Lauderdale. He died August 31, 1969, in a plane crash near Newton, Iowa, and is buried in Fort Lauderdale at Forest Lawn Memorial Gardens–Central.

Ingemar Johansson, who defeated Floyd Patterson but lost twice to him later, retired to Lighthouse Point. He bought and operated the Sea Cay Motel in Pompano Beach.

NETBALL

The influx of British expatriates and immigrants from Caribbean nations—particularly Jamaica—has fueled an interest in netball, a derivative of old-style women's basketball. The west-central part of Broward County is the hottest spot for netball action and several tournaments are held annually.

In July 2005, Broward County became the hotspot of the netball world for almost three weeks when the Broward County Convention Center hosted the Fifth World Youth Netball Championships for women's under-twenty-one teams from around the globe.

More than twenty teams participated in the competition, bringing more than five hundred athletes. The American team, predictably, was an early casualty. When all the dust cleared, Australia and Jamaica, the top two seeds, were on the bench for the championship match, which pitted number three New Zealand against England. The Kiwis prevailed, 53–39.

Rodeo

Western Broward has been the site of several rodeos, but two have existed on a long-term basis. One is the Seminole Rodeo. The other is the town of Davie's rodeo program, held at the Bergeron Rodeo Grounds.

Davie—originally called Zona—hosted its first rodeo in 1923. In 1946 a handful of town ranchers, cowboys and cattlemen cobbled together the first rodeo arena in town. The town planned to raze the arena in 1978, but the town's horse-loving citizens organized a protest and town council members listened. Local businesses, led by Ron Bergeron, a rodeo cowboy inducted into the Broward County Sports Hall of Fame in 2006, ponied up funds to improve the arena area. A roof was built over the arena and Bergeron dug deep to pay for land for parking, landscaping and paving.

Soap Box Derby

In 1961 Gary Patchen, of Wilton Manors, finished second in the All-America Soap Box Derby in Akron, Ohio. In 1998 Patchen's son Greg, of Merritt Island, finished second in the Masters Division at Akron.

Soccer

The Fort Lauderdale Strikers and the teams that followed in their wake helped introduce soccer to the American public and nurture the game. While in Fort Lauderdale from 1977 to 1983, the Strikers introduced

Rodeo has long been a part of life in Davie. In this picture, Chris Love rushes to the aid of Gator Smith at the Davie Rodeo Arena. *Broward County Historical Commission, Sun-Tattler collection. Photo by Catharine Krueger.*

many international stars to new American soccer fans: Branko Segota, goalie Jan van Beveren, midfielder Teofilo "Nene" Cubillas, striker Gerd Muller, George Best, Ray Hudson and Gordon Banks. The team's most memorable year was 1980, when it went all the way to the league's championship, the Soccer Bowl, losing to the New York Cosmos. The Strikers also helped grow the sport from youth leagues up in Broward, Dade and Palm Beach Counties, with players teaching frequent clinics, coaching elite youth games and making appearances at soccer venues.

The United Soccer League was formed in 1984 after the collapse of the American Soccer League II. Fort Lauderdale, hurting after the departure of the Strikers, was a natural city to introduce the team and became home to the Fort Lauderdale Sun. A few familiar names, such as goalie Jim Tietjens and field players Keith Weller and Ernst John-Baptiste remained.

Nine teams made up the USL in its first year. The Sun dominated throughout, winning the Southern Division and prevailing over the Houston Dynamos in the three-game champion series, 1–2, 2–1 and 3–0.

In the second year, the league, for the most part, had folded, but four teams remained, and the Sun tweaked its name to South Florida Sun. The league folded shortly before the start of the second half of the second season. South Florida led in the standings with a 4–2 record.

The following are soccer players of note from Broward:

Mark Chung, a graduate of Cooper City High, went into professional soccer, playing for the Tampa Bay Mutiny, Colorado Rapids, New York MetroStars and has played for the U.S. national team more than two dozen times.

Teofilo "Coquito" Cubillas, Jr., son of Nene Cubillas, the Strikers' superlative midfielder, grew up in Coral Springs, graduated from Nova Southeastern University and was selected by the Miami Fusion in the 2001 MLS Super Draft.

Miljce Donev went on from Stranahan High to the College of Boca Raton (now Lynn University), then to professional soccer. He played with Hershey of the AISA and played midfield for several years with the Fort Lauderdale Strikers of the American Professional Soccer League.

Alvin James was a fleet-footed forward for Boyd Anderson High and was named an all-county player his junior and senior years. He went on to Florida International University for two years, then to the University of North Carolina at Greensboro. Finally, he went on to play professionally for the Fort Lauderdale Strikers during their years as part of the American Professional Soccer League.

Peter "Sneaky Pete" Marino, a native of Pompano Beach, played soccer at Brevard Community College and Bayer Leverkusen's amateur squad in Germany, then played professionally for SC Brouck in Germany's third division as well as several MLS teams including the Columbus Crew, Miami Fusion, Kansas City Wizards, Tampa Bay Mutiny and D.C. United.

Zenon Luzniak was the leading scorer for his four years on Cooper City High's soccer team, earning all-county, all-state and All-America honors. He went on to play a year at Wake Forest before injuries took him out of the game. He rehabbed with a Dutch professional team and felt at home in the professional atmosphere. He went on to play professionally, including a stint playing midfield and striker for the Fort Lauderdale Strikers during their years in the American Professional Soccer League.

Tyrone Marshall was born and spent his early years in Jamaica, but moved to Lauderhill at age twelve. He went on to play at Florida International University and then went into Major League Soccer, playing defender for the Miami Fusion, Colorado Rapids and the Los Angeles Galaxy.

When the Marjory Stoneman Douglas High Eagles sought their fourth consecutive state soccer championship in 2006, Lake Mary High seemed ready to dethrone them. The teams battled to double overtime tied, 1–1. With time running out and a shootout looming, *Brianna Schooley* launched a long shot—about 22 yards out—that gave the Eagles their fourth state championship in a row, 2–1. Schooley scored 154 goals and added 87 assists in her years at Douglas. She was named Miss Soccer by the Florida Dairy Farmers in 2005 and 2006, was named the 2005 Player of the Year by the National Soccer Coaches Association of America and a member of the NSCAA/Adidas Girls High School All-America team in 2005. She also was also a three-time first-team all-state team member. She went on to play at the University of Central Florida.

Mark Schwartz played soccer professionally and was named the United Soccer League's Rookie of the Year in 1984, playing for the Fort Lauderdale Sun.

Circumstance sent *David Winner* to soccer. "My dad took me to register for T-ball and they were all full," he said. "Soccer was registering right next to it and that's how I started in Margate Youth Soccer."

He never left. His father later moved to Cooper City, giving Winner the chance to play goal for club teams in Pembroke Pines and Sunrise, and for Western High under the guidance of Coach Gary Coleman. After Western, Winner went on to Florida International University and the University of Tampa. Following that, he bounced around professional soccer. His favorite stop was for the Miami Fusion: "It was a great experience because I grew up watching the Fort Lauderdale Strikers and [Dutch goalkeeping great] Jan van Beveren in that stadium, even if it had a facelift. It was great to play in front of my friends and family, and my first game was against the [Columbus] Crew, who I played for three years...and we won!" Winner currently is the goalkeeping director for the Austin United Capitals soccer program in Texas.

Softball

Broward County was once the white-hot core of the slow-pitch softball universe, but as slow-pitch—a hitter's game—gave way to fast-pitch—where pitchers dominate—the softball scene in Broward cooled a degree or two, but still remains hot.

Steve Nicosia, right, confers with Mike Simons at Fletcher Park. *Broward County Historical Commission, Sun-Tattler collection.*

The Fort Lauderdale Gators were probably the first team to attract national attention, when they won the 1971 Amateur Softball Association of America Women's Major Open National Slow Pitch championship. Louise Crocco, who went on to become Cardinal Gibbons High's athletic director, was the Gators' pitcher and was named a first-team All-America player as a result of her play in the tournament. Other Gators named to the All-America first team were Karren "Sparky" Newman, who hit .435 and played third base, and Ernestine Hamel, who hit .571 and played outfield. The tournament MVP was also a Gator, Donna Phillips, who also hit .571. The Gators went 7–0 at the national tournament.

For youth programs, Broward remains a softball hotbed, but no area is hotter than Pembroke Pines, whose program is an object of envy nationwide. Behind the leadership of Bucky Strickland, former Pittsburgh Pirates catcher Steve Nicosia and an army of volunteers, the Pines program became a national model.

The eight-and-under *Lil Thunder* program won the national championship in 1998, a Southern National championship in 1999 and the International Softball Association world championship in 1999.

The *Mighty Midgets* program, for players ten and under, won Amateur Softball Association of America national championships in 1987, 1990, 1991 and 1993. In 1988, 1989, 1992 and 1994, they won world titles.

The ten-and-under *Thunder Red* team won the National Softball Association's national championship in 2000.

The twelve-and-under *Pacers* won national championships in 1984, 1985, 1986, 1989, 1990, 1992 and world championships in 1993 and 1994.

The fourteen-and-under *Thunder* won national titles in 1989, 1990, 1991, 1992 and a world title in 1993.

The sixteen-and-under *Cardinals* program won ASA national titles in 1975, 1983, 1984, 1985 and 1987 and a world championship in 1988.

The *Thunder* 16B team was the National Softball Association's 2004 national champion.

The eighteen-and-under *Bandits* were world champions in 1986.

In the late 1980s and early 1990s, the Pembroke Lakes *Swampfrogs*, of Pembroke Pines, a program for boys, also was nationally prominent. The Swampfrogs won the ASA's boys fifteen-and-under slow-pitch national title in 1982, 1985 and 1993. The Swampfrogs also won the sixteen-and-under national crown in 1986 and the national sixteen-to-eighteen title in 1986.

Wakeboarding

The second annual U.S. Cable Wakeboard National Championships were held at Ski Rixen at Quiet Waters Parks in Deerfield Beach, and the 2006 Cable Nationals were held at Ski Rixen as well. Cable skiing and wakeboarding are fairly common in Europe, but there are only a handful of cable ski facilities in the United States.

Yacht Racing

The Whitbread Round the World Yacht Race (now the Volvo Ocean Race), from its start in 1972 was the world's premier yacht race. The race took the name of its sponsor, Whitbread PLC, and was contested every four years.

The first race started on September 8, 1973 in Portsmouth, England, with stops in Cape Town, South Africa; Sydney, Australia and Rio de Janeiro, Brazil, concluding in Portsmouth. In 1989–90 and 1993–94, the race started and ended in Southampton, England, with two stops in Punta del Este, Uruguay and one stop each in Freemantle, Australia; Auckland, New Zealand and Fort Lauderdale.

For the 1997–98 race, Fort Lauderdale remained one of the stops and Cape Town and Sydney were added back in. Other cities added were San Sebastiao, Brazil; Baltimore/Annapolis, Maryland; and LaRochelle, France.

Fort Lauderdale was dropped and replaced by Miami for the 2001–02 race.

6

Swimming

In the city later to be known as the Venice of America, early swimming competitions were not held at the beach, but in New River. In a 1924 swimming race, for example, five swimmers (August Burghard from Fort Lauderdale, two brothers from Dania and two other boys) ages fifteen and sixteen, dove off the Andrews Avenue bridge at high tide and headed east toward the ocean. A small outboard motorboat accompanied them. The spectators packed picnic lunches and as the swimmers began their 3.5-mile race, they sped off toward Colee Hammock for lunch as they awaited their arrival. The women set out homemade picnic lunches, complete with lemonade, as the children played games and the men pitched horseshoes and played board games.

After the swimmers passed Colee Hammock, the leftovers were packed up and the spectators headed to see the swimmers arrive at the finish. In 1997 a distance race along the same route was held as a fundraiser. One athlete completed the race.

For those who preferred swimming in tamer, safer surroundings, Francis Abreu designed the Las Olas Beach Casino at A1A and Southeast Fifth Street. The complex was the first Olympic-sized pool in the state and opened in 1926. The 60-by-165-foot saltwater pool was a technological marvel for its time—it completely purged and changed water every ten hours. The first Collegiate Aquatic Forum—a winter swimming extravaganza that allowed college swimmers the opportunity to practice and compete in sunny Fort Lauderdale while their classmates were slogging through snow at home during the holiday break—was held in 1935.

The pool complex, popularly known as the casino pool, was demolished in 1966 after the International Swimming Hall of Fame Aquatic Complex opened its doors across the street in 1965. Since then, the complex has hosted a variety of national and international swimming, diving, water polo and synchronized swimming events. The complex underwent extensive renovations in 1989. At the west end of the complex property is the International Swimming Hall of Fame, a historic and educational museum commemorating the accomplishments of the greatest competitors and coaches in swimming, diving, synchronized and marathon swimming and water polo.

For a while, most notably in the early 1980s, Fort Lauderdale became the center of the marathon swimming universe, in large part because of the influence of Buck Dawson, the International Swimming Hall of Fame's founder and director for its first two decades, who brought an increased focus on swimming to Fort Lauderdale.

Diana Nyad, who swam around Manhattan, from the Bahamas to Florida, as well as the English Channel, and Stella Taylor, a multiple English Channel crosser who also swam Lake George and Lake Okeechobee, were the headliners, but there was a fine supporting cast as well, featuring the "Tiger Twins" (brothers James and Jonathan diDonato), who failed in an attempt to butterfly-stroke their way across the English Channel together, and Dawn Chovan, who succeeded in setting a record for swimming twenty-four consecutive hours of the backstroke in the Fort Lauderdale High School pool in December 1981. Nyad (1978), Taylor (1982) and Dawson (1993) were all inducted into the International Marathon Swimming Hall of Fame.

Hollywood also had a casino pool as the center of its aquatic endeavors. The pool, opened during the 1930s, was at Johnson Street at the Broadwalk. Billy Outten, one of the local children who swam and dove for the pool's youth team, became a professional diver.

Coral Springs opened its aquatic center in 1989, and like the Hall of Fame pool, it has become a training and international competitive site.

Listed are some more swimmers and divers to come from Broward County:

Bradley Ally was a St. Thomas Aquinas student when he represented his native Barbados at the 2004 Olympic Games at Athens. Ally swam in four events and set personal records in three of them.

Andy Coan followed a tradition of excellence as a sprinter, winning the state Class 3A fifty-yard freestyle championship in 1973–76 and the hundred in 1973–75. As a high schooler at Pine Crest, he broke Mark Spitz's hundred-meter freestyle world record. He won three gold medals in the 1975 World Championships. Spitz went on to compete at the University of Tennessee, where he won seven NCAA championships. Coan was among the charter honorees of Pine Crest's Athletic Hall of Fame in 1983 and the Broward County Sports Hall of Fame in 2006.

During his heyday in the 1960s, *David Edgar* was the fastest man on water. A Fort Lauderdale High swimmer coached by Jack Nelson, Edgar won the state fifty-meter freestyle in 1967 and '68 and the one-hundred-meter freestyle in 1968. Then he blazed to a national scholastic record of 21.2 seconds in the fifty-meter freestyle. By the time he got to the University of Tennessee, he had established himself as America's premier short-course sprint specialist. Edgar took NCAA championships in the fifty and one hundred freestyle for the University of Tennessee in 1970, '71 and '72; he also set a United States record in the fifty, with a 20.5 effort against Navy. His coach, Ray Bussard, described him as "the fastest man afloat." In 1972 at Munich, Edgar became the first Volunteers swimmer to win Olympic gold as a member of the world-record-setting four-hundred-meter freestyle relay team. He also finished fifth in the hundred-meter butterfly. He won gold in the Pan American Games, the Amateur Athletic Union national championship in the hundred-meter freestyle and seven NCAA national championships. He was inducted into the International Swimming Hall of Fame in 1996.

Evan Linette, a three-time state scholastic champion at Fort Lauderdale High, rose to the top of junior diving in the United States, winning eight junior national titles and being named to the Junior World team twice and the Junior Pan Am team. After going on to compete at the University of Texas, he quit diving at eighteen and returned home to enroll at Broward Community College to become an airline pilot.

Ann Marshall, a member of Pine Crest's class of 1975, where she won multiple state championships and was named a high school All-America. She went on to the University of North Carolina, where she received the university's first women's swimming scholarship.

A case of viral endocarditis ended *Diana Nyad*'s hopes of making the 1968 Olympic swimming team, but gave birth to her astounding career as a distance swimmer. Nyad went on from Pine Crest to Lake Forest College in Chicago, where she played on the Foresters' tennis team. She resumed swimming while there, only concentrating on distance events.

After graduating from college, she returned to Broward to train under distance swimming guru Buck Dawson, where her ability and drive made her a phenomenon. The seventies were Nyad's heydays as the world's top distance swimmer, which included swims across Lake Ontario, around Manhattan Island, the Suez Canal, Nile River, Bay of Naples, Great Barrier Reef and a 102.5-mile, two-day trip from the Bahamas to Florida in 1979.

In the 1980s, she went from being covered by the media to a member of it. Over the years she has worked for NBC, ABC Sports, Fox Sports, National Public Radio and more.

Nyad, Olympic swimmer Andy Coan and water-skiing champion Wayne Grimditch were among the charter honorees of Pine Crest's Athletic Hall of Fame in 1983. Nyad is also a member of Lake Forest College's Athletic Hall of Fame. She was inducted into the National Women's Sports Hall of Fame in 1986 and the International Swimming Hall of Fame in 1993.

Vladislav Polyakov's journey has been a long one, from his native Kazakhstan to St. Thomas, the University of Alabama and into international competition. He represented Kazakhstan in the 2004 Olympics in Athens, setting national records in the one- and two-hundred-meter breaststroke. In 2006 he won Kazakhstan's first swimming medal at Doha 2006, by winning the fifty-meter breaststroke in the Asian Games.

At five feet two inches, *Katherine "Katy" Rawls* was a tiny zephyr, zipping through the water at the casino pool, the saltwater facility just east of where the International Swimming Hall of Fame pool now stands. The oldest of Bill and Sadie Rawls's water-loving offspring, Katy Rawls was born in Nashville but spent her early years in central Florida and began swimming in the lakes there, then headed south to Broward County, where she graduated from Fort Lauderdale High School.

Rawls was born before the era of specializing in certain events, so her accomplishments in the pool were wide-ranging. In freestyle, she swam distances from the sprints right up to the mile. She also swam the individual medley, the breaststroke, in relays and dove from the platform and springboard. All told, she won thirty-three national championships and two Olympic silver medals in springboard diving and a bronze medal in the four-by-one hundred freestyle relay. She was among the twenty-one athletes in the first group to be inducted to the International Swimming Hall of Fame in 1965.

Paige Zemina is another of the many great swimmers who developed under the tutelage of Jack Nelson. She was a high school All-America swimmer at St. Thomas Aquinas, and an NCAA All-America at Florida. She won a bronze medal in the two-hundred-meter freestyle at the 1986 Goodwill Games, was on the two-hundred-meter freestyle relay team that set a world record (1:43.50) at a USS international meet at the University of Arkansas in 1985 and won an Olympic bronze medal as part of America's four-by-one-hundred meter free relay team in 1988.

Pam Kruse's moment in time lasted nearly two years. The Pompano Beach High School student set two world records in the four-hundred-meter freestyle in an eight-day period in 1967, starting with a 4:36.8 effort at Fort Lauderdale on June 30, then a 4:36.4 effort at Santa Clara, California, on July 7. She represented the United States in the 1968 Olympics at Mexico City, where she finished second in the 80-meter freestyle in a time of 9:35.7.

7

Tennis

Even without Chris Evert, tennis would have been wildly popular in Broward County. The sport has a rich history in the area, lots of courts and a climate that allows players plenty of days of sunshine and temperate weather each year.

But because of Christine Marie Evert, tennis reigns in Broward. The oldest daughter of Jimmy and Colette Evert, Chris took naturally to the game under the watchful eye of her father, who had played the game at Notre Dame. All the Evert children played tennis at varying levels of the game; none played it as well as Chris.

The oldest Evert child was Drew, born in 1953. He graduated from St. Thomas Aquinas High and went to Auburn University on a tennis scholarship. He went on to work as a club professional in Charlottesville, Virginia. He now works as director of adult programs and tournaments at the Evert Tennis Academy in Boca Raton.

Jeanne, who was born in 1957, also graduated from St. Thomas Aquinas. She joined the women's tour after high school and played professionally through 1978. Highlights of her career included slots on the U.S. Wightman and Federation Cup teams. She also served as director of tennis at Stonebridge Country Club and director of teaching at the Delray Beach Tennis Center. She married Braham Dubin, a Canadian accountant who went on to start tennis and golf management and development companies. They had two children: daughter, Catherine, and son, Eric. Braham Dubin received a kidney transplant in the late seventies. He died September 10, 2006, in Boca Raton.

Brother John, born in 1961, broke the mold and went to rival Cardinal Gibbons High. A Junior Orange Bowl champion and perennial top-ten junior, he went on to Vanderbilt University, where he was captain of the men's tennis team and received a degree in economics in 1994. He worked for International Management Group first as an agent, then as vice-president of its Racquet Sports Division, from 1984 to 1993. From 1993 to 1996, he worked as general manager of the Harry Hopman Tennis Academy then went on to join Chris on the staff of the Evert Tennis Academy, in Boca Raton, where he serves as executive director and director of player development.

The baby of the Evert clan is Clare, born in 1968. Tall and muscular, Clare seemed to possess all the gifts a tennis player needed to thrive. She revived the family history by going to St. Thomas Aquinas High, then struck out for Southern Methodist University. Like her siblings, she found her way back to Florida and directed the Chris Evert Pro-Celebrity Tennis Classic.

Chris was the second child, born on December 21, 1954, in Fort Lauderdale. She graduated from St. Thomas Aquinas High and turned pro on her eighteenth birthday.

She won the 1971 S&H Green Stamps Classic, defeating Laurie Fleming, 6–2 and 6–1, and made her pro debut at that same tournament in 1973, which she also won. She also played the 1971 Virginia Slims of Fort Lauderdale and the 1972 Women's International, also in Fort Lauderdale. With Evert as the headliner, tournaments in Broward and throughout South Florida were slam-dunk successes.

Take for example the Lynda Carter/Maybelline Classic, a tournament that ran for four years at the Deer Creek Tennis Center in Deerfield Beach. Evert won three of the four years, losing only to Andrea Jaeger, 4–6, 6–3 and 6–0, in 1981. She beat Jaeger twice in the finals and in the other, beat Bonnie Gadusek, 6–0 and 6–4.

Other Broward-based tournaments Evert played included the S&H Green Stamps Classic (Fort Lauderdale, 1974), Virginia Slims of Florida (Hollywood, 1977) and the Avon Championships of Florida (Hollywood, 1979).

Outside Broward, her legend grows. Evert was ranked number one in the world for seven years. She won 1,309 matches in her seventeen-year professional career, which ended with a 7–6, 6–2 loss to Zina Garrison in the quarterfinals of the 1989 U.S. Open. She held a win average of .904.

Among her victories were 157 singles titles and 18 Grand Slam titles. With clay as her favorite playing surface, it's no surprise that seven of those titles were earned on the clay at Paris' Stade Roland Garros. From 1973 to 1979, she won 125 consecutive matches on clay.

The one area of tennis where Evert never really clicked was the Olympics, but she only got one shot at them. She represented the United States at the Seoul Games in 1988. Elise Burgin was bumped from the U.S. team's roster to accommodate Evert, but Evert lost to Italy's Raffaella Reggi before the medal round.

Off the court, Evert was romantically linked with Steve Ford, Burt Reynolds and Adam Faith, engaged to Jimmy Connors, married twice and stalked at least once. One man was barred from watching Evert play in the Ford Challenge Cup at PGA National in Palm Beach Gardens in 1985 after sending Evert more than two hundred love letters. Another of Evert's lovelorn male admirers—a navy veteran from Michigan—broke into her home at the Polo Club in Boca Raton on June 13, 1987. Evert was not in the country at the time of the break-in. The offender was caught at a nearby restaurant with a stack of love letters addressed to Evert in his possession.

Evert's first marriage was to British player John Lloyd. They married April 11, 1979, at St. Anthony's Catholic Church in Fort Lauderdale. They were divorced in 1987. Her second marriage was to former Olympic skier Andy Mill. They were married July 30, 1988, at the Polo Club in Boca Raton. That marriage resulted in three sons: Alexander, Nicholas and Colton. On October 20, 2006, Mill and Evert announced that after eighteen years of marriage, they planned to divorce.

Even before her competitive days concluded, Evert showed she wished to use the stature she had attained in tennis as a platform for other good works. She formed the Chris Evert Charities and has raised millions to fight drug abuse through an annual tournament, the Chris Evert Pro-Celebrity Tennis Classic. She works as a TV tennis commentator and with her family owns and operates the Evert Tennis Academy in Boca Raton's Mission Bay neighborhood. In June 2006, the center was designated the USTA's player development center.

A few more of the dozens of outstanding tennis players to come out of Broward County include:

As the world's top-ranked junior in 1990, *Ivan Baron* rarely lost, but representing Plantation High in the 1990 state singles champion, he lost in the finals to Vimal Patel, of Haines City, 6–2, 3–6 and 6–2. As a professional, he was ranked 218th, and at the end of his playing career went into promoting tennis events with his father, Mark.

Herbert "Buddy" Behrens won three singles and three doubles Florida High School Activities Association championships for Fort Lauderdale Hugh School. He went on to play for Rollins College, from where he graduated in 1951. He was named to the Tars athletic hall of fame in 1994. In 1947 he was ranked number one in the national junior singles rankings and went on to win the national junior singles and doubles championships that year. He is a member of the Broward County Athletic Hall of Fame.

Always intense and tenacious, *Jay Berger* became the national eighteens champion and Florida's 1985 clay court champion. After graduating from Plantation High, he played two years at Clemson before turning pro and played for the U.S. Davis Cup team before winning the U.S. Clay Court title in 1989. Berger later coached at the University of Miami, where he led the Hurricanes to the Big East conference championships in 2000 and 2001, where he was twice named Big East Coach of the Year. Berger now works as a USTA national men's coach in Key Biscayne.

Hollywood Hills grad *Laura Bernstein-Kassirer* went on to the University of South Carolina, where she was a two-time All-America before turning pro in 1983. She made five appearances at Wimbledon and later founded the Youth Tennis League, a national organization devoted to providing tennis educational and competitive opportunities for youths.

Cardinal Gibbons grad *George Bezecny* went on to the University of Georgia, where he played on the 1985 NCAA champion men's tennis team with Mikael Pernfors.

Jennifer Capriati was born in New York and as a toddler her father, Stefano, had her hitting ground strokes at the local tennis center. The Capriatis moved to Lauderhill, where Jennifer worked with Jimmy Evert at Holiday Park. She made her pro debut not long before turning fourteen and has had an up-and-down career. The highlight of her career to date was defeating Steffi Graf in three sets to win the 1992 Olympic gold medal in Barcelona.

Dan Cassidy played in high school at Hollywood Hills and went on to play for Auburn. He was named to the 1984 Junior Davis Cup team and won a USTA circuit tournament at Mobile in 1989.

The Fleming family: Fred Fleming was a three-sport athlete at California University of Pennsylvania and who won eleven varsity letters. He was inducted into CUP's athletic hall of fame in 1997. His tennis-loving family consisted of his wife, Norma, daughters, Laurie and Carrie, and son, Scott. Laurie finished second in the state singles championships twice and runner-up in doubles once with Sandra Trice. She went on to play on the Virginia Slims professional tour. She married S. Pike Rowley and they are the parents of a daughter, Carrie, and son, Brett.

Carrie Fleming played on Gibbons' team, too, finishing second with Elisa Padula in the 1972 doubles championship. She went on to Trinity University, where she was named to the All-America team.

Lisa "Lele" Forood: The 1974 state singles champion from St. Thomas Aquinas High, Forood went on to Stanford, when she was named an

Daniella Ghizdavu in 1985. *Broward County Historical Commission, Sun-Tattler collection. Photo by Vincent J. Ferraro.*

All-America in 1976. After graduating from Stanford, she was ranked as high as thirtieth on the women's pro tour, but found she enjoyed working behind the scenes better. She went on to work for the Women's Tennis Association from 1979 to 1987 and won the WTA Player Service Award in 1983.

She returned to her alma mater to serve as an assistant coach. In 1997 she was named the Interscholastic Tennis Association's Assistant Coach of the Year. In 2000 Stanford's Frank Brennan retired and Forood was appointed to replace him. Since then, she has led the Cardinals to a new level. The Cardinals won the NCAA team title in a 30–0 season. She also posted undefeated seasons in 2004 and 2005. In 2003 she was named the Wilson/ITA National Coach of the Year.

Daniella Ghizdavu went from Hallandale High to BCC, where she was one of the Seahawks' early tennis All-America players. She was one of six players named to the All-America squad in 1987.

Jamie Golder teamed with Lisa Sassano to win the FHSAA doubles championship in 1979 for Piper High. Golder went on to play as number one for the University of Miami before turning pro.

Brian Gottfried, a graduate of Piper High School, played for Trinity University then went into the pros, where he won $2,781,614 in career prize money. He worked several years as director of tennis at St. Andrew's Country Club in Boca Raton, where served as its first tennis director and touring pro. There he coached players such as Greg Holmes, Luke Jensen, Jay Berger and Carling Bassett.

Tall and powerful, *Dana Kanell* was an impressive figure on the tennis courts for Westminster Academy. She and teammate *Angela Bernal* won the FHSAA Class 2A doubles championship in 1987. Kanell got her athletic genes from her dad, orthopedic surgeon Dan Kanell, who served as team physician for the Florida Marlins, Miami Dolphins, New York Yankees and other athletic teams, and shares her athletic talents with her brother, NFL quarterback Danny Kanell.

Steve Kennedy went to the University of Miami after graduating from Cardinal Gibbons High and played the Israel pro circuit in 1986.

Mark Merklein of Coral Springs is a native of Freeport, Grand Bahama Island, and has played for the Bahamas in Davis Cup play. In January 2006, he was named to the USTA's national coaching staff's men's program, but left before the end of the year to become James Blake's fitness trainer and workout partner. A graduate of the University of Florida who won the 1994 NCAA singles championship for the Gators and teamed with David Blair to

Steve Rayner became the teaching professional at Pembroke Lakes Racquet Club after his touring career ended. *Broward County Historical Commission, Sun-Tattler collection. 1989 photo by Joel Stahl.*

win the 1993 doubles championship. Merklein played on the pro tour from 1994 to 2005. He is a member of the University of Florida Hall of Fame. He reached the quarterfinals at the 2000 Olympics at Sydney, Australia and also competed in the 2004 Olympiad at Athens.

Shenay Perry, a native of Washington, D.C., moved with her family to Coral Springs when she was eleven so she could train year-round. Her father, Ron Perry, was Shenay's first coach and went on to become a coach for the city of Fort Lauderdale's parks and recreation department. Perry skipped college and the international juniors circuit to go pro. By 2006 she had reached a ranking of forty-third.

Felicia Raschiatore of Coral Springs High needed only two quick sets to defeat Michael Weis of Pinellas Park, in order to earn the FHSAA girls singles championship in 1979. She went on to play at Trinity, sampled the pro tour and then became a teaching pro.

Steve Rayner was born in Miami but grew up in Broward and attended Chaminade-Madonna College Preparatory. He spent three years in Port Washington, New York, studying and honing his game with Australian legend Harry Hopman. Rayner joined the men's pro tour in 1971 and stayed there until 1976, with highest ranking as 150.

Joey Rive, a native of Hato Rey, Puerto Rico, grew up in Fort Lauderdale, where he worked with coach Craig Wittus at the Tennis Club. He played at Florida State University, where he majored in psychology.

Joelle Schwenk is in the FHSAA record book for her four state titles—three in doubles and one in singles. After Gibbons, Schwenk went on to play for the University of Kentucky.

Piper High graduate *Robert Seguso* went on to Southern Illinois University at Edwardsville. He and Ken Flach were America's toughest doubles team on the pro circuit. He married Canadian pro Carling Bassett.

Harold Solomon came to Fort Lauderdale from Maryland in time to reach the number one singles slot on Fort Lauderdale High's 1969 state champion team. He teamed with *Gilbert Theissen* to win the state doubles crown. Solomon went on to Rice before joining the pro tour. He amassed twenty-two tour victories and served as the president of the Association of Tennis Professionals for five years. After his touring days ended, he became a teaching pro and has coached many highly ranked players such as Justin Gimmelstob, Mary Joe Fernandez and Anna Kournikova.

Like her brother, Harold, *Shelly Solomon* went on to a career in tennis, but each took separate paths to get there. She went to Piper, where she won the 1980 state singles championship, then played 1981–82 at UCLA before turning pro.

Slobodan Zivojinovic, the Yugoslavian pro nicknamed "Bobo," was for a while a part-time resident of Broward, owner of a winter home in Lighthouse Point.

8

High School Heroes

Boyd Anderson High School

Boyd H. Anderson High School is in Lauderdale Lakes. The school's teams are nicknamed the Cobras.

Don Blackmon has shown considerable staying power in the NFL, both as a player and coach. After completing his career at Boyd Anderson, he went on to play at Tulsa from 1976 to 1980, where he made 336 tackles playing defensive end. He established the university's record for tackles with losses with 40 for -239 yards. He was named the Missouri Valley Conference's Defensive Player of the Year in 1980, and also was second team All-America in 1978 and 1980. He was inducted into Tulsa's Golden Hurricanes Hall of Fame in 1989.

Blackmon was the 102nd player selected in the 1981 NFL draft, taken by the New England Patriots in the fourth round. He went on to play linebacker for the Patriots from 1981 to 1987, including Super Bowl XX in 1985. A quarter of the way through the 1987 season, he suffered a career-ending neck injury.

Blackmon remained with the Patriots after his playing days ended, first spending one year as a staff assistant, then two years as the linebackers coach. Short stints at Cleveland and the New York Giants followed. From 1997 to 2000 he served as linebackers coach for the Atlanta Falcons, which included a trip to Super Bowl XXXIII. He ended his Atlanta career after a year as the Falcons' defensive coordinator. Blackmon then spent 2003–05 in Buffalo, two of those years working under Northeast

High grad Mike Mularkey. Blackmon joined the Kansas City Chiefs' coaching staff in 2006.

Asante Samuel could do it all for the Cobras. He played quarterback and defensive back on the football team, rushing for more than 500 yards and passing for more than 1,600 in his senior year. He also played baseball and basketball for his school. He went on to play football at the University of Central Florida, where he started at free safety as a freshman and sometimes even stepped in as quarterback. The next year he went to cornerback and found his home there. He was selected by the New England Patriots in the fourth round of the 2003 NFL Draft, 120th overall. In his first season, he started against former Taravella High School star Dan Morgan in the Patriots' 32–29 victory over the Carolina Panthers in Super Bowl XXXVIII. Other Cobras football players reaching the National Football League are *Abdul Hodge*, a linebacker for the Green Bay Packers, *Benny Sapp*, a cornerback for the Kansas City Chiefs and wide receiver *Todd Devoe*, who played on the Baltimore Ravens' practice squad.

Mitch Richmond, a transfer from Deerfield Beach High, became the Cobras' top basketball alum. Richmond began playing basketball at Deerfield Beach's Park Apartments, alongside Dixie Highway, then took his game to Westside Park. He left Deerfield Beach High for Boyd Anderson after his freshman year. After high school, he went on to Kansas State. From there he played for the U.S. Olympic men's basketball team, where he was a starter. Richmond was drafted in the first round by the Golden State Warriors.

Floyd Miley played a big role in the game ranked seventy-fifth among college football's hundred greatest finishes. Miley, a defensive back for the University of Tennessee, picked up a blocked kick and ran it back eighty-five yards for a touchdown to help turn around a 31–7 deficit to Notre Dame, en route to a 35–34 victory over the Fighting Irish.

For *Alvin James*, please see the Soccer section in Sports of All Sorts.

Attucks High School

Attucks High was the public high school serving South Broward's black communities during the days of segregation. Attucks was converted to a middle school in 1968.

All-purpose athlete *Cyril Pinder* played three sports—football, basketball and track—at Attucks and three positions on the football team: running back, defensive back and linebacker. As a senior, he won the shot put, finished second in discus and third in both the high jump and hundred-yard dash at the state track meet. Pinder went on to play at Illinois and played eight years in the NFL, with two seasons with the Chicago Bears and stops with the Philadelphia Eagles and Dallas Cowboys. He rushed for 1,709 yards in his NFL career.

Cardinal Gibbons High School

Cardinal Gibbons High School was established in 1961. For many years Gibbons teams were known as the Redskins, but the mascot changed to the Chiefs in 2006.

"Be true to your school," an old Beach Boys tune advises, and *Louise Crocco* certainly has, coaching her volleyball teams to seventeen state championships between 1972 and 2003 and leading the school's athletic program to excellence. Crocco also was an acclaimed athlete, selected a 1971 all-America pitcher by the Amateur Softball Association of America as part of the Fort Lauderdale Gators national champion slow-pitch team. After completing her education at Broward Community College and Florida Atlantic University, Crocco returned to her alma mater to coach girls' sports and later became the school's athletic director. She is the winningest coach in the state of Florida and was named National Coach of the Year by the National Federation of State High School Associations and the National Federation of Interscholastic Coaches. Cardinal Gibbons' tennis program has sent many players off to colleges and a few into the pro ranks.

Donnell Bennett began playing football near his home in Pompano Beach and went on to play in the Pompano Chiefs program, which started him up the ladder to stardom. He went on to Cardinal Gibbons, then to Miami. He was drafted fifty-eighth overall, late in the second round of the 1994 NFL draft, by the Kansas City Chiefs. Bennett played nine years in the NFL—seven for Kansas City and two for the Washington Redskins. Over that period he rushed for 1,941 yards and caught passes totaling 352 yards. Bennett returned home before the start of training camp during summer with fellow NFL players to host a summer camp for local youths planning to play high school or youth football.

Jim Gurzynski was Gibbons's first athlete to letter in three sports. He chose baseball to pursue and went on to Broward Community College and Florida State, then into the majors in the Dodgers organization. Gurzynski was one of the first four members inducted into Gibbons' athletic hall of fame.

Ryan Shealy played basketball, baseball, football and volleyball for the Redskins. He won a variety of accolades; his baseball prowess earned him a slot on the Collegiate Baseball TPX All-America team. By the time he got to the University of Florida, it was baseball that had won over his heart. In his senior year, he hit .379 with twenty-three homers and drove in seventy-three runs.

The Colorado Rockies selected him as a first baseman in the eleventh round of the 2002 Major League draft. He moved up through the Rockies' farm system with stops in Tulsa, where he was named to minor league baseball's Fab Fifty for 2004. Shealy made it to the Rockies' parent club, but was traded to Kansas City to play first base and serve as a designated hitter.

Fred Buckley went on to play quarterback at Stanford. In the 1984 season he was the Cardinals' starter, completing 81 of 166 passes for 940 yards and five touchdowns.

Mark Van Zwieten simply followed in the shoes of his brothers Steve and Jim, but had one distinct advantage: men's volleyball didn't become a varsity sport in Florida until 2003. He was a member of the 2005 team that went 31–0 and won the state championship, setting records for service aces in a match (eight) and in a tournament (seventeen). Now, Van Zwieten, whose brothers Steve and Jim have played on the Association of Volleyball Professionals tour, plays with the big boys, too. He and brother Jim placed second in the AVP Pro Wild Card Championship in Tampa Bay in June 2006. In August 2006, he participated for the United States team for the Swatch-FIVB Under-21 World Volleyball Championships in Myslowice, Poland.

William "Skeeter" Zimmerman, a 2003 Redskins graduate, spent a few of his early years in Hawaii and learned to surf there. After graduating from Gibbons, he began surfing pro events. Among his conquests were the overall championships at the Treasure Coast Pro-Am in Stuart, top spot in the Pro-Am Division of the Jupiter Pro Fall Classic and number one at the National Scholastic Surfing Association Southeast-North College Conference championships.

For Cardinal Gibbons graduates *George Bezecny*, *John Evert*, *Carrie Fleming*, *Laurie Fleming*, *Steve Kennedy* and *Joelle Schwenk*, please see Tennis.

Chaminade-Madonna College Preparatory

Chaminade High School and Madonna Academy were established in 1960. In 1988 the schools merged to form Chaminade-Madonna. The school's teams are nicknamed the Lions.

At five feet seven inches and 170 pounds, *Bill Capece* was a multi-sport athlete for the Lions, running track, playing baseball and becoming a standout running back and kicker for the football team. As a senior, Capece ran for eight hundred yards and ten touchdowns. He was comfortable in the world of sports because his father, Vince, worked as a scout for the California Angels. His kicking ability is what took him to the next level in sports. He went on to kick for Florida State and was named first team *Sporting News* All-America in 1980. He scored 108 points in a Seminoles uniform and played in two Tangerine Bowls and one Orange Bowl game. He was drafted by Houston in the twelfth round of the 1981 NFL draft and later signed as a free agent with the Tampa Bay Buccaneers. He kicked for three years with the Bucs, scoring 196 points. He was named to the FSU Athletic Hall of Fame in 1990. After leaving football, Capece went into law enforcement, working with the Leon County Sheriff's Department in Tallahassee.

The player who served as Capece's holder at Chaminade didn't do badly, either. *David Shula*, son of Miami Dolphins coach Don Shula, was named to all-county baseball and football teams and salutatorian of his class. He went on to Dartmouth College, where he was named New England Football Player of the Year in 1980. He was signed as a free agent by the Baltimore Colts in 1981 and spent a year there as a kick-return specialist and wide receiver. He joined the staff of the Miami Dolphins under his father. He stayed with the Dolphins through 1989, when he joined the staff of the Dallas Cowboys. In 1991 he was named an assistant coach with the Cincinnati Bengals, and in 1992 became the Bengals' head coach at thirty-two, the youngest head coach in NFL history. He coached the Bengals until 1996, building a record of 19–52. After leaving the NFL, Shula became executive vice-president of Shula's Steak Houses. David Shula's oldest son, Dan, went on to play quarterback at St. Thomas Aquinas and followed his father to Dartmouth.

Chris Godfrey went on to play nine years on the offensive line for the New York Giants. He was the starter at right guard on the 1987 team that won Super Bowl XXI. Godfrey is probably better known for his post-playing years. He became an attorney and is founder and president of Life Athletes, a group of more than three hundred professional athletes attempting to teach moral and ethical lessons to America's youth.

Coconut Creek High School

Coconut Creek High School was established in 1973. Its teams are nicknamed the Cougars.

After *Darrell McClover* made sixteen sacks as a senior for the Cougars, it was clear great things lurked in his future. He went on to play for the University of Miami then was drafted in the seventh round of the 2004 NFL draft by the New York Jets. He played in sixteen games on special teams for the Jets in 2004 and made twelve tackles in the limited time he had playing linebacker. An ankle injury that required surgery kept him out of the 2005 season and he was cut in 2006 spring training. McClover was picked up by the Chicago Bears in October 2006 and played in the Super Bowl in front of family, friends and his high school coach, Grantis Bell.

For *Steve Rayner*, see Tennis.

Cooper City High School

Cooper City High School was established in 1971. Its teams are nicknamed the Cowboys. Its original mascot was a cartoon character called Pistol Pete, but Pete was replaced with Lasso Larry because guns he carried were deemed inappropriate symbols for the school.

Even though the school is in the southwestern part of the county, Cooper City was one of the state leaders in water polo with the efforts of Lee Childs, who retired in 2003 after nearly thirty years at the school. Under his leadership water polo has grown throughout the state and the Cowboys won a men's state title in 1992 and a women's state championship in 1994.

Olindo Mare has spent most of his professional life working a short drive from where he attended high school, but it took a long road to get there. After graduating from Cooper City, he went on to Valencia Community College, which had no football program. He moved next to MacMurray College in Jacksonville, Ill., then to Syracuse University for his final two

Opposite: In a 1985 photo, Lee Childs sits on a starting block as he instructs his water polo team. *Broward County Historical Commission, Sun-Tattler collection. Photo by Mark Edelson.*

SWIMMING

years, where he hit fifteen of twenty-four field goals and was named to the All-Bid East second team.

Mare was signed by the New York Giants as an undrafted rookie free agent and spent the 1996 season on their practice squad. After he was waived, the Dolphins picked him up for the 1997 season through the present. His breakout year came in 1999, when he had the most prolific season of any Dolphins kicker. He hit thirty-nine of forty-six field goal attempts, including a long kick of fifty-four yards.

Wide receiver *Robert Thompson* played college ball at Youngstown State, then was drafted in the sixth round (142 overall) by the New Orleans Saints in the 1986 NFL draft.

For former Cowboys *Mark Chung* and *Zenon Luzniak*, see the Soccer section in the Sports of All Sorts chapter.

CORAL SPRINGS HIGH SCHOOL

Coral Springs High School was established in 1975. Its teams are nicknamed the Colts.

Guard *Steve Hutchinson* is regarded as possibly the best offensive lineman in pro football in 2006, and certainly he's among the best paid in the

University of Tennessee quarterback Brent Schaeffer looks for a receiver in a game against the College of the Sequoias. *College of the Sequoias Sports Information Office.*

league at his position as well as an all-Pro player. After graduating from Coral Springs, Hutchinson went on to the University of Michigan and was then drafted number seventeen in the first round of the 2001 NFL draft by the Seattle Seahawks. He played from 2001 to 2005 in Seattle then went to the Minnesota Vikings in 2006.

Leatha Ingram was better known as "Lisa" and was a dominant figure on the basketball court wherever she played. After leaving Coral Springs, where she was a two-time All-America, she went on to Northeast Louisiana State University, where she scored fifty-two points against Louisiana State University. She made the NCAA All-America team in 1985 and is a member of the university's athletic hall of fame. After playing internationally and on the U.S. Pan American team, Ingram returned to Broward County. She was inducted into the Broward County Sports Hall of Fame in 2006 and now coaches basketball at Coral Glades High.

For *Felicia Raschiatore*, see Tennis.

Deerfield Beach High School

Deerfield Beach High School is located in the northeast quadrant of Broward County, not far from the border with Palm Beach County. The school's teams are nicknamed the Bucks.

As the adage goes, when life gives you lemons, make lemonade. *Stockar McDougle*, who began playing football in the Deerfield Raiders program before going on to Deerfield Beach High, found himself at Navarro Junior College in Corsicana, Texas, so he twice made Junior College (JUCO) All-America teams, then signed with Oklahoma and earned his way to the NFL, where he has played on the offensive line for the Jacksonville Jaguars, Miami Dolphins and Detroit Lions. He and his brother Jerome, an Ely grad who plays for the Philadelphia Eagles, created the McDougle Brothers Foundation to aid Broward youths.

Derrick Crudup's father played his high school football just north of Broward's county line, at Boca Raton High, but Derrick Jr. was a Buck all the way. Derrick Sr. started his college career at Florida before transferring to Oklahoma and going on to the NFL, but despite a quarterback controversy, Derrick Jr. played his entire college career at Miami. After college, he played for the Spokane Shock of Arena Football 2, throwing passes to former Plantation wide receiver Kevin Beard.

Brent Schaeffer made history, then history turned sour on him. Schaeffer, a University of Tennessee football player, was on top of the world when he became the first true freshman to start at quarterback in the Southeastern Conference since 1945. He remained the starter for two more games, then lost the job. Things got worse after he was suspended from the team after being arrested following a dormitory altercation. Schaeffer enrolled at College of the Sequoias, where he directed the top JUCO offense in the nation. Following the year in Visalia, California, he moved on to Ole Miss, where he was the starter for the 2006 season.

DILLARD HIGH SCHOOL

Dillard High School opened in 1950. Its teams are nicknamed the Panthers.

At Dillard, extraordinary athletes are an ordinary occurrence, but *Lorenzo White*, by any measure, was special. At Michigan State, he was a two-time All-America and finished fourth in Heisman voting in 1985 and 1987. He was drafted in the first round of the 1988 NFL draft by the Houston Oilers, where he spent seven seasons, including a Pro Bowl year in 1992. He also spent one year with the Browns. In all he rushed for 4,242 yards on 1,062 carries, scoring 30 touchdowns. He also made 192 receptions for 1,738 yards and 6 touchdowns.

Percy Leonard Howard had a short yet meaningful career in the NFL. After leaving Dillard, he went on to Isothermal Community College and Austin Peay as a basketball player, but his leaping ability and good hands got him notice with the Dallas Cowboys. He spent the 1975 season with the Cowboys, but was only used sparingly, returning two kickoffs during the season and catching one pass—for a thirty-four-yard touchdown from Roger Staubach as the Cowboys pressed in the waning moments of Super Bowl X against the Steelers. The catch was the only one of Howard's NFL career.

Wide receiver *Isaac Bruce* was another of the highly motivated, physically gifted athletes to use Dillard as a steppingstone to the next level, but the road for Bruce wasn't all that smooth in spots. After helping the Panthers reach and win the 1989 Class 5A state championship, he headed off to college, attending West Los Angeles and Santa Monica Junior College before hooking on with Memphis State. He completed his collegiate career with 113 catches for 1,586 yards and 14 touchdowns. Bruce was made the thirty-third draft pick of the 1992 draft by the Los

Football is king at Dillard. In this 1987 picture, Dillard's Leon Thompson, left, attempts to drag St. Thomas Aquinas's Bobby Lawson for a few extra yards in a clash between the two football titans. Lawson went on to become St. Thomas's baseball coach. *Broward County Historical Commission, Sun-Tattler collection.*

Angeles Rams and has remained in a Rams uniform through the present. In his first twelve years with the Rams, he caught passes for more than 12,000 yards and 77 touchdowns.

Charles Leo "Charlie" Goodrum went from Dillard to Florida Agricultural and Mechanical University (FAMU) and then was drafted in the ninth round of the 1972 NFL draft. He spent seven years in the NFL, all of them for the Minnesota Vikings as an offensive lineman. Goodrum was inducted into FAMU's Athletic Hall of Fame in 1993 and the Broward Sports Hall of Fame. Another Panthers player who went to the pros via FAMU was *John Kelly*, a tackle, who played from 1966 to 1967 with the Washington Redskins. A more recent Dillard-FAMU connection to the pros was quarterback *Quinn Gray*, son of legendary Dillard coach Otis Gray, who went from FAMU to the Jacksonville Jaguars as an undrafted free agent. Other Panthers who went on to the NFL are *Calvin Jackson*, *James Bostic*,

Lorenzo Davis, Herman Smith, Bobby Scott, Hyland Hickson, Isaac Brown, James Adderley, Ernest Adams, Leonard Myers, Claude Jones, Charles Dorsey, Tron LaFavor, Jason Davis, Asa Francis, Chris Gamble, Matthias Askew, Fred Miller, Johnny Lamar, Gregory Brewton and *Frank Sanders. Otis Mounds*, a defensive specialist who went on to Auburn University, played seven years in Arena Football. *Kevin Jackson*, a wide receiver and linebacker who played at Tennessee State, played three years in the AFL. *Maurice Dix* also played on the Florida Bobcats with Jackson. *Wendal Lowery* and *Jerald Boyd* played football in Europe.

On the hardwood, *Keyon Dooling* transferred from Cardinal Gibbons to Dillard to play his senior year with buddy *Clarence Gilbert*. Both went on to Missouri together and into the pro ranks, but from there, their roads differed. Gilbert, a point and shooting guard, didn't stick in the NBA, so he went abroad, playing for teams such as Bosnia ASA HBTelecom in the Adriatic Basketball Association and Istanbul Darussafaka of the Turkish Basketball League. Dooling played four years for the Los Angeles Clippers, a year for the Miami Heat and as of 2006 was playing for the Orlando Magic.

MARJORY STONEMAN DOUGLAS HIGH

Marjory Stoneman Douglas High, named to honor the environmentalist and author, opened in 1990 in Parkland. The school's teams are nicknamed the Eagles.

Shortstop *Mike Caruso* was selected by the San Francisco Giants in the second round of the 1996 amateur baseball draft. He was sent to the San Jose Giants and in 1997 was traded to the Chicago White Sox. He became the White Sox's starting shortstop in 1998 and batted .306. He played there one more year and one year (2002) for the Kansas City Royals.

Mark Zupan, who played football and soccer for the Eagles, seemed to have his future all mapped out. An honor student and athlete, his soccer-playing ability had earned him a full-ride scholarship to Florida Atlantic University, but fate intervened. Zupan was napping in the back of a friend's pickup when the friend drove away—unaware Zupan was in the back. The truck was involved in an accident. Zupan was ejected and suffered a neck fracture that left him quadriplegic. After his injury, Zupan, who went on to Georgia Tech and earned a degree in civil engineering, got involved in the hard-hitting, not-for-the-timid world of wheelchair rugby, where he earned a bronze medal in quad rugby for the United States in the 2004 Paralympics in Greece. Zupan also became the focus of a film about quad rugby—*Murderball*—which made him a celebrity. Zupan wrote a book that was released in October 2006 and Coral Springs proclaimed November 21, 2006 as Mark Zupan Day.

For Eagle *Brianna Schooley*, see the Soccer section in the Sports of All Sorts chapter.

Blanche Ely High School

Blanche Ely High School opened in Pompano Beach in 1952. Its teams are nicknamed the Tigers.

Alshinard "Al" Harris played quarterback and cornerback for the Tigers in their golden years, with *Henri* and *Zack Crockett*, *Tyrone Carter* and *Corey Simon*, but when the Crockett boys and Simon went to Florida State, and Carter went to Minnesota, Harris headed off to Trinity Valley (Texas) Community College, then to Texas A&M—Kingsville. Still he made his mark in the Lone Star State, capping his career at Kingsville with eighty-eight tackles, sixty-one of them solo.

Harris was drafted in the sixth round by the Tampa Bay Buccaneers (169th overall) in the 1997 NFL draft. He went to the Eagles in 1998 after being waived. He played for Philadelphia through 2003, when he was traded to Green Bay.

Harris owns several businesses in South Florida. He lives now in Coral Springs and sponsors a Pompano Cowboys team annually.

Henri and *Zack Crockett* played together in high school and at Florida State, then went their separate ways in the NFL. Zack, the older of the brothers, ran for 481 yards as a fullback at FSU and was a third-round pick of the Indianapolis Colts. He later went on to the Raiders. Henri, an outside linebacker, played on FSU's 1993 national championship team. He was drafted by the Falcons and then played for the Vikings.

The brothers now operate the Crockett Foundation, based in their hometown of Pompano Beach. The foundation provides academic and athletic opportunities for disadvantaged youth in South Florida.

Tyrone Carter, a free safety, ran for 1,344 yards and 23 touchdowns as a senior for the Tigers. He also broke free on kickoff returns of 90, 95 and 97 yards. He then went on to Minnesota. There he twice won the Carl Eller Award as defensive player of the year. As a defensive back, he racked up 528 tackles, won the Jim Thorpe Award and was a first team All-America and all–Big Ten player.

He was selected in the fourth round of the 2000 draft by the Vikings, the 118th pick overall. During his pro career, he has played for the Jets, Steelers and Vikings.

Corey Simon is a hunter. His prey is quarterbacks. After being named Broward's defensive player of the year by the *Miami Herald*, he packed his bags for Tallahassee and Florida State, where he was a finalist for the Lombardi Award and Outland Trophy. Simon was the sixth overall pick in the 2000 draft by the Philadelphia Eagles, where he has gone on to be one of the NFL's sack masters, the fourth Eagles defensive tackle to reach twenty-five sacks.

Off the field, his interests lie in helping youth. He created the Corey Simon Success Center in Tallahassee to help enhance the lives and educational opportunities for underprivileged youths in the Big Bend area.

James Jones came to Ely High when it reopened in 1978 and played two seasons there, leading the Tigers to a district title in 1979. He moved on to the University of Florida, where he amassed 2,018 yards on 486 carries and 17 touchdowns. He was the top pick of the Detroit Lions in the 1982 NFL draft. He also played for the Seattle Seahawks. In all he spent eleven years in the NFL, rushing for 3,626 yards and 36 touchdowns. After his playing days ended, he went into coaching, first at Wharton High in Tampa. In February 2007, he was named Ely's head coach.

Defensive end *Jerome McDougle*, brother of Deerfield Beach High grad Stockar McDougle, continued his education at the University of Miami, where he was an all–Big East selection and a Lombardi Award finalist. He was the first pick of the Philadelphia Eagles in the 2003 NFL draft. He spent most of his first two years in the NFL injured. At the start of the 2005 season he was shot in the stomach during a robbery attempt at the start of training camp. However, he recovered and returned for the 2006 season.

Charles W. Flanagan High School

Flanagan High, which opened in 1996, is named in honor of the founding mayor of Pembroke Pines, where the school is located. The school's teams are nicknamed the Falcons.

A three-time all-Broward selection for the Falcons, *Nick Turnbull* later ended up playing for another Falcons team—the Atlanta Falcons of the NFL. At Florida International, he became the Golden Panthers' all-time interceptions leader, with sixteen picks. He became FIU's first player to play in an NFL regular-season game in November 2006, when he was moved up from the Falcons' practice squad to play on special teams for the Falcons against the Browns. Turnbull went to the Falcons as an undrafted free agent in May 2006.

Fort Lauderdale High School

Broward County's first high school, Fort Lauderdale High opened with a class of five boys in 1918. The school's teams are nicknamed the Flying L's. Originally Fort Lauderdale's teams did not have a nickname and wore only a simple "L" on their jerseys. At a track meet, one Fort Lauderdale runner was performing well beyond his rivals prompting a spectator to gasp, "Look at that Flying L go!" A newspaper reporter heard the remark, used it in his story and the nickname stuck.

Though he never played basketball professionally, *Charles Martin "C.M." Newton* made significant contributions to the game on many levels. A 1948 graduate of Fort Lauderdale High, Newton was a three-time all-state basketball player for the Flying L's who went on to play at the University of Kentucky, where he was a member of Adolph Rupp's 1951 NCAA championship team that went 32–2. Blessed with an endorsement from Rupp, Newton went on to coach basketball at Transylvania, Alabama and Vanderbilt, compiling a career record of 509–375. He was a four-time Southeastern Conference (SEC) coach of the year and led Alabama to three SEC titles. He also served as assistant commissioner of the SEC, team manager for the 1984 U.S. Olympic basketball team and athletic director at Kentucky from 1989 to 2000, where he made historic hiring choices that crossed the color barrier. Additionally he served as president of USA Basketball from 1992 to 1996, chairman of the USA Basketball Games Committee from 1988 to 1992, and a member of the International Basketball Federation (FIBA) Central Board from 1994 to the present. Newton was named to Kentucky's Alumni Hall of Fame in 1998, and enshrined in the Basketball Hall of Fame in 2000.

Alexander "Sandy" Nininger was a gangly football player for the Flying L's in the late 1930s. He went on to West Point, where he graduated in 1941. With World War II raging, he was sent to the Philippines. At Abucay, Bataan, on January 12, 1942, armed only with a rifle with bayonet and some hand grenades, Lieutenant Nininger, twenty-three, slipped behind

Scot Shields during his days at Lincoln Memorial University. *Lincoln Memorial University Sports Information Office.*

enemy lines to eliminate soldiers hiding in foxholes and tree positions. He was wounded three times before suffering fatal wounds. Lieutenant Nininger was posthumously awarded the first Congressional Medal of Honor of World War II on January 29, 1942.

Scot Shields learned to play baseball in the Wilton Manors Little League, then continued playing when he went across the bridge from the Island City to Fort Lauderdale High, where his mother, Ida, worked. His father and grandfather played in minor leagues, and they passed their abilities down the line. A durable, right-handed relief pitcher, Shields was drafted in the thirty-eighth round by the Anaheim Angels in the 1997 MLB first-year player draft, and has stayed in the organization. Called up from AAA Salt Lake to the parent club in June 2002, Shields pitched in Game Five of the 2002 World Series against the Giants, losing 16–4. He gave up five runs in one and two-thirds innings, including a pair of home runs.

Evette Young helped establish Fort Lauderdale as the team to beat in girls' flag football. The Flying L's won the first state championship in the sport in 2003, defeating Lake Worth, 14–7, in the championship game. Young set the individual rushing record that year, running for 161 yards on 20 carries versus Apopka.

The middle son of an accomplished Fort Lauderdale sporting family, *Chuck Zloch* went on to attend Notre Dame as his brothers Bill and Jim did. Unlike his brothers, who went into law, Chuck played defensive back for a few years for the Detroit Lions (Bill, a Central Catholic grad, become a judge and Jim, a Flying L, became an attorney).

For the Flying L's champions in the pool—*David Edgar*, *Evan Linette*, *Katherine "Katy" Rawls* and *Harold Solomon*—see Swimming.

Hallandale High School

Hallandale High School opened in 1973. Its teams are nicknamed the Chargers.

Donald "Butch" Rolle: After his career with the Chargers ended, Rolle went on to Michigan State, where his career included 57 catches for 604 yards, but was far better known for his blocking ability. He went to the NFL, where he played for six years with the Buffalo Bills and two years with the Phoenix Cardinals. In all he caught 38 passes for 213 yards and 11 touchdowns.

For *Daniella Ghizdavu*, see Tennis.

Hollywood Hills High School

Originally called Stirling High, Hollywood Hills High's teams are nicknamed the Spartans.

Richard "Keith" Uecker earned nine letters at Hills, then went off to Auburn, where he excelled on the Tigers' offensive line, becoming an all-SEC and All-America player his senior year. He was awarded the Ken

Keith Uecker during his days at Auburn University. *Auburn University Sports Information Office.*

Rice Award, given to Auburn's top offensive lineman, for his junior and senior years. Uecker was drafted in the ninth round, 243rd overall, by the Denver Broncos in the 1982 draft. After two years at Denver, he went to the Green Bay Packers, where he found his home. He started for four years there, playing guard and tackle, and worked as an accountant in the off-season. He was named recipient of the Ed Block Courage Award in 1987. Uecker went into college coaching after his pro career ended. He worked at the University of Akron for five years and joined the staff as offensive line coach at Wayne State in 2004.

Adrian Jones at the University of Missouri. *University of Missouri Sports Information Office.*

Adrian Jones got a worldview of professional football few have enjoyed. After graduating from Hills, where he played halfback and defensive back on the football team and also was a standout in baseball, drafted by the Cincinnati Reds. He went on to play four years of college football at Missouri, where he played alongside prep teammate *Charles Murphy* in the Tigers' secondary. By his senior year, Jones, who played cornerback, was one of four Tigers featured on the 1989 Mizzou press guide's cover. He ended his career with the Tigers as their all-time interceptions leader with sixteen and started forty consecutive games.

His professional career saw him in three leagues: one, with the Cincinnati Bengals (1992), two with the Saskatchewan Roughriders (1995–96) and two years (1991–92) with the Barcelona Dragons of the World League of American Football. The Dragons drafted Jones in the second round of their first draft, and he responded with three interceptions in his first year. The Dragons went on to the 1991 World Bowl in London, where they lost to the London Monarchs, 21–0. In the league's second (and final year), Jones was named to the all-league team at cornerback.

Dexter Nottage, born in the Bahamas, went on from Hollywood Hills to Florida A&M, where he played defensive end and defensive tackle for the Rattlers. He spent 1994–1996 on the Washington Redskins' roster and the 1997 season played one game for the Kansas City Chiefs.

Bill Voeltz, a hard-throwing lefty closer for the Spartans took his blistering fastball to Broward Community College, St. Thomas University and then into minor-league baseball, pitching for A and AA teams in the New York Yankees' organization. Voeltz became an ordained youth minister after an injury ended his baseball career and was shot to death in Jupiter, Florida, in May 2006. He was forty-two.

For *Laura Bernstein-Kassirer* and *Dan Cassidy*, see Tennis.

MCARTHUR HIGH SCHOOL

McArthur High School is in Hollywood. Its teams are known as the Mustangs.

On a football Friday night in the late 1980s, *Errict Rhett* was a little slow climbing off the Mustangs' bus. He'd gotten engrossed in a book and didn't want to put it down. "I was doing a little reading," he said, almost sheepishly, holding the book up slightly so his guest could see it. It was a well-worn copy of the Bible. Rhett explained reading it before a game or a wrestling match calmed him down, kept him focused. Rhett went on to lead the Mustangs to a 10–0 season in 1988, the first unbeaten season in school history.

Rhett went on to play for the University of Florida, where he racked up 4,163 rushing yards and 1,230 receiving yards. He was drafted thirty-fourth overall, a second-round selection of the Tampa Bay Buccaneers in the 1994 NFL draft. He spent four years in Tampa Bay, two with the Baltimore Ravens and five games with the Cleveland Browns, before a foot ligament injury ended his season and ultimately his playing career. Rhett ran for 4,143 yards on 1,174 carries as a pro, scoring 29 touchdowns.

Oddibe McDowell Jr. played football, baseball and wrestled for the Mustangs, but left his mark in the outfield, playing baseball first at Miami-Dade Community College, then at Arizona State, where he won the 1984 Golden Spikes Award. In the summers, he played for the Alaska Goldpanners, where he hit .322 in 1982 and .350 in 1983. He competed for the United States on the 1984 Olympic team. He was picked as the twelfth overall selection in the 1984 amateur draft by the Texas Rangers and turned pro, spending nine years in the Majors, with stops in Texas, California and Atlanta. He was named to the Broward County Sports Hall of Fame in 1999.

Bryant McFadden left McArthur headed for Florida State rated as the top prep prospect in the country. By the time he left Florida State, he had successfully continued a tradition of All-America cornerbacks. McFadden was drafted in the second round of the 2005 NFL draft, the thirtieth player chosen overall by the Pittsburgh Steelers.

Jamaica-born *Damion McIntosh* wrestled and played football and baseball at McArthur and all that conditioning helped him at Kansas State, where he played offensive and defensive tackle. He's playing in front of family, friends and old classmates now as a Miami Dolphin, after being made a free agent by the San Diego Chargers, who drafted him in 2000.

Miramar High School

Miramar High School was opened in 1973. Its teams are nicknamed the Patriots.

Recreation, physical education, law enforcement and sociology are common college majors for football players, but not for *Dean Biasucci*. After leaving Miramar for Western Carolina, he chose a major football players generally eschew—theater.

After being bypassed in the NFL draft, Biasucci signed as a free agent with the Atlanta Falcons in 1984. After he was released, he hooked on with the Colts, who used him as a kickoff specialist, then released him the following year. He spent 1985 out of football. The Colts called again in 1986 and he became their kicking specialist for the following nine seasons. He ended his tenure with the Colts as their leading scorer—783 points—and was a Pro Bowl selection in 1987. His final year in professional football was 1995, when he kicked for eight games with the St. Louis Rams. In all, he scored 825 points in the NFL.

After football, Biasucci put his education to work, appearing in films such as *Jerry Maguire*, *Boa*, *Rustin* and *Madison* and TV shows such as *ER* and *The West Wing*. He then returned to North Carolina, where he is a businessman and still appears in regional theater.

Jesse Bendross went on from Miramar to Alabama, where he played split end and flanker for the Crimson Tide from 1980 to 1983, catching 76 passes for 1,359 yards and nine touchdowns. He was the 174th pick of the 1984 NFL draft, going to the San Diego Chargers, where he played wide receiver for two years and part of one season for the Philadelphia Eagles.

Clarence Coleman racked up 8,009 career all-purpose yards at Ferris State University and was named a consensus first team preseason All-America in 2001 for the Bulldogs. He was a finalist for the Harlon Hill Trophy, given to the NCAA Division II player of the year. He led the Division

Jesse Bendross during his years at Miramar High. *Broward County Historical Commission, Sun-Tattler collection.*

II records for total yards with 4,983, and catches with 323. Coleman played flanker and split end at Ferris State. He spent part of 2003 with the Buffalo Bills, was a wide receiver and defensive back for the Grand Rapids Rampage of the Arena Football league and played for the Florida Frenzy in the National Indoor Football League.

Lisa Pinkney-Bowles was a top track performer for the Patriots in the sprints and middle-distance events. She won the state four-hundred-meter scholastic championship from 1978 to 1981. She went on to attend and compete at Southern University. She was named to the Broward County Sports Hall of Fame in 1999.

For *Mark Schwartz*, see the Soccer section of the Sports of All Sorts chapter.

Northeast High School

Northeast High School is in Oakland Park. Northeast's teams are nicknamed the Hurricanes.

You can go home again. *Mike Mularkey* has proved it, covering the spectrum of football after playing quarterback for the Hurricanes, he went on to the University of Florida, where he lettered for three years. He was drafted in the ninth round of the 1983 draft by the 49ers and played tight end for the Vikings and Steelers. He caught 102 passes in 114 NFL games, for 1,222 yards and nine touchdowns.

After his playing career ended, he began coaching at Concordia College in 1993 as the offensive line coach. He moved to the NFL the next year as a quality control coach for Tampa Bay. He spent eight years on Steelers coaching staff and was named head coach of the Buffalo Bills in 2004, where he compiled a record of 14–18. He resigned after the Bills fired five of his assistants and hired Marv Levy as general manager. A week after leaving the Bills, he was appointed offensive coordinator of the Miami Dolphins in 2006.

Glenn Adolpho set a state high school volleyball tournament record for most kills in the state tournament (83) and is tied for first for most kills in a single match (34), both set in 2004. He was selected in 2006 for the United States team at the Swatch-FIVB Under-21 World Volleyball Championships in Myslowice, Poland.

After graduating from Northeast, *Grantis Bell* became a walk-on at West Virginia, where he played from 1985 to 1988 and became an all-East receiver. After college, he made his way through the pros, playing for the New York Jets in the NFL, the Detroit Drive. Massachusetts Marauders and the Tampa Bay Storm of the AFL and the Orlando Thunder of the World League of American Football. After his playing days ended, Bell became a coach, first at Coconut Creek High, then became an assistant athletic director at Fort Lauderdale High.

Terry Richardson left Northeast for the cooler climate of upstate New York at Syracuse University, where he carried the football for 1,523 yards on 307 carries. After college, he was signed to a free-agent contract with the Cincinnati Bengals in 1994, followed by stints with the Philadelphia Eagles, Kansas City Chiefs and Pittsburgh Steelers. After ending his playing career, he returned home to Northeast to serve as offensive coordinator/running backs coach for a year, then accepted a position as running backs coach for the University of Connecticut.

Nova High School

Created as part of the South Florida Education Center in Davie, Nova High School opened in 1960. Its teams are nicknamed the Titans.

Autry Denson once held Broward's all-time rushing record, with 4,738 yards. He went on to Notre Dame, where he played defensive back for a while, then went back to the offensive backfield. By the time he left the Fighting Irish, he was Notre Dame's leading rusher, with 4,318 yards on 854 carries and 43 touchdowns. Professionally, he played for the Tampa Bay Buccaneers, Miami Dolphins and Detroit Lions, but made his biggest splash as the feature running back for the Rhein Fire in NFL Europe. Denson got the Fire off to a smashing start in 2003 with three successive hundred-yard games.

Denson's teammate *Khalid Abdullah* went on to Mars Hill College and was drafted with the first pick of the fifth round of the 2003 draft by the Cincinnati Bengals, where he played the season at linebacker.

Warren Holmes, a wide receiver and kick returner, went on to achieve junior college All-America before playing for the Tampa Bay Bandits of the United States Football League.

For *Mike Donald*, see Golf.

Pine Crest School

Pine Crest School of Fort Lauderdale was established in 1934. Its athletic teams are nicknamed the Panthers.

After playing decades of football and sending players on to some of the finest colleges and universities in the nation, the Panthers finally had a player drafted by the NFL in 2006. Offensive lineman *Kevin Boothe* went to the Oakland Raiders with the sixth pick in the sixth round, number 176 overall. Named first team All-America by the American Football Coaches Association and the NFL Draft Report, Boothe showed he was tough as nails. At Cornell in his sophomore year, Boothe, a medical redshirt, played with fractures in both hands. Boothe became the fourth Big Red player to earn all-Ivy honors three times in his career. At Pine Crest, Boothe excelled on both sides of the ball and was a first team all-county and second team all-state pick. *Charles Boothe*, Kevin's brother, played football at East Carolina University, and Boothe wore number 77—his brother's number at ECU—at Pine Crest and Cornell.

H. Wayne Huizenga played center for the Panthers football team during his student days, but made a bigger splash several decades later as owner of the Miami Dolphins, Florida Marlins and Florida Panthers. He later sold the Marlins and Panthers.

Wayne Grimditch was the ironman of water skiing. He left behind a string of accomplishments in his fifteen-year career in the sport that will be difficult to surpass. He jumped 169 feet in the 1972 Masters for a world record, and in 1975 topped 180 feet for another. He is the first jumper to hold records in the Junior Boys', Boys' and Men's divisions at the same time.

He was a member of the U.S. National team in 1969, 1971, 1973 and 1975. In all, he set ten national jumping records and four world marks. But Grimditch, who began tournament skiing at eight in 1963, qualified for his first national tournament a year later. At that competition, he won national titles in jumping and tricks and finished third in slalom.

Grimditch also was a Class 2A all-state football player for the Panthers, but found his greatest glory and exposure in winning the 1978 ABC Superstars competition, a made-for-TV sports extravaganza that brought together a slate of the country's top athletes in a variety of sports.

For *Andy Coan*, *Ann Marshall* and *Diana Nyad* see Swimming.

Piper High School

Piper High School, named for aviation pioneer and entrepreneur William Thomas Piper, was opened in Sunrise in 1972. Its teams are nicknamed the Bengals.

Speed thrills, and flashy *Brian* and *Bennie Blades* had plenty of it. Both went on to record-setting careers at the University of Miami and careers in professional football. Brian Blades played wide receiver for the Hurricanes from 1984 to 1987. He then went on to twelve years in the NFL with the Seattle Seahawks.

Bennie Blades was an All-America safety in 1986 and 1987 and co-winner of the Jim Thorpe Award in 1987. He played eleven years in the NFL with the Detroit Lions and the Seattle Seahawks and has been inducted into the College Football Hall of Fame.

Bobby Harden, who played safety at the University of Miami, was drafted in the twelfth round of the 1990 draft by the Miami Dolphins, where he played for four years.

Quadtrine Hill, son of former Miami Dolphins running back Eddie Hill, inherited his dad's speed and moves. An all-state tailback for the Bengals, Hill ran for 1,356 yards and went on to Miami, where he was converted to running back and also played some at fullback and on special teams. Hill spent stints with the Houston Texans and Chicago Bears in 2006.

Frances Savage, who scored 30.5 points and pulled down fifteen boards per game as a senior for the Bengals went on to become the University of Miami's first marquee player for its women's basketball team. A Converse All-America and all-state player in high school, she was a Proposition 48 player at UM, meaning she sat out her first year, but once she got on the court, showed her greatness. By her senior year, Savage was featured on the UM press guide cover. She finished her UM career second all-time in scoring, with 2,184 points and first in scoring average with 23.2 points per game and was a Kodak All-America selection. She also played for Team Florida in Korea. Savage went on to become a supervisor for customs and border protection for the Department of Homeland Security.

For *Jamie Golder*, *Brian Gottfried*, *Robert Seguso* and *Shelly Solomon*, see Tennis.

PLANTATION HIGH SCHOOL

Plantation High School opened in 1963. Its teams are nicknamed the Colonels.

The Colonels traditionally wear red and white uniforms, but *Ryan Schneider* was their golden boy, passing for 5,005 regular-season yards. The Colonels, under coach Frank Hepler, were one of the area's dominant teams and Schneider's maturation as a player was accelerated, no doubt,

Kevin Beard whoops it up as a member of the Spokane Shock. *Spokane Shock.*

through the attention of his father, Carl, who served as the Colonels' offensive coordinator.

After being sought by the University of Hawaii, West Virginia University, Auburn University, the University of Florida and the University of Central Florida, Schneider decided to stay near home and his family and girlfriend to play at Central Florida. For much of his career, he seemed to epitomize the Golden Knights, setting up to make an assault on Duante Culpepper's passing records. But during his senior year, he violated a team rule and was suspended for the last few games of the season. He ended his career at UCF with 10,976 yards passing, for eighty-two touchdowns, both second to Culpepper. After his UCF career ended, he earned a tryout with the Tampa Bay Buccaneers but was released late in the 2003 training camp. He went on to earn a slot on the Arena Football League Orlando Predators' roster, but a shoulder injury ended his season early. From there, he went to the Tennessee Valley Vipers of the Arena Football 2 league (AF2), then on to the Odessa Roughnecks of the Intense Football League, where he appeared in three games, completing 22 of 29 passes for 186 yards and a pair of touchdowns.

Kevin Beard, who was on the receiving end of many of Ryan Schneider's passes, still holds Broward County's record for touchdown receptions in a single season, with sixteen. He was nearly as good on the basketball court, averaging 18.3 points per game, earning him second team all-state honors. Beard went on to play at the University of Miami, where he made 67 receptions at flanker for 920 yards and seven touchdowns. He was part of the Hurricanes' 2001 national championship team that defeated Nebraska in the Rose Bowl. After college, Beard played a year for the South Georgia Wildcats of Arena Football 2, then went on to the expansion Spokane Shock. "He has been a pleasure to have on our team," said Shock general manager Adam Nebeker.

Al Blades, younger brother of Bennie and Brian Blades, was a defensive back for the Colonels and the University of Miami, where he roomed with Beard and won the team's Hard Hitter Award. He was named to the All-Big East first team in 2001. Blades was a passenger in a car that struck a bridge abutment and plunged into a Miami canal in March 2003. Blades, twenty-six, drowned.

Kevin Timothee lettered in football and track for the Colonels, then went on to Ole Miss, where he did not play his freshman year. He decided to transfer to Florida International's new program and became the first Golden Panther player to sign a professional contract. He played three seasons at cornerback at FIU, making 42 tackles. He was signed by the Tennessee Titans as an undrafted free agent, but released before the start of the 2005 season. After a few days in the New York Giants' camp, he was cut loose again. He was drafted in the third round of the 2006 NFL Europe draft by the Amsterdam Admirals.

James Hurst, who went on to Florida Southern College after graduating from Plantation, was drafted by the Texas Rangers and started eight games for the Rangers in 1994.

For *Jay Berger* and *Ivan Baron*, see Tennis.

POMPANO BEACH HIGH SCHOOL

Pompano Beach High School was established in 1926, then closed in 1985 as the population migrated westward. Teams from the school were originally nicknamed the Beanpickers to reflect the community's agricultural roots. In 1958, the nickname was changed to Golden Tornadoes. Pompano Beach High School reopened as an all-magnet high school in 1997.

Thanks to one fateful play, *Barry Krauss* is frozen forever in time and the memories of Alabama and Penn State fans, but all he had longed for was to play for the Miami Dolphins. In Mrs. Sayers' third-grade class at McNabb Elementary School, he wrote an essay describing his desire to play for the Dolphins. Little did he know then that he'd play for two of the legendary coaches of the sport—Don Shula and Paul "Bear" Bryant.

In addition to football, Krauss played baseball and ran track for the Tornadoes. He also competed statewide in the decathlon.

He signed with Alabama and became a Crimson Tide legend for his all-out tenacious play and for one play in particular in the 1979 Sugar Bowl game. The Crimson Tide was leading number one Penn State, 14–7. At fourth-and-goal from the one-yard line, the Nittany Lions gave the ball to Mike Guman. Krauss drove through the Penn State offensive line and stood him up; teammate Don McNeal hit him low and together they denied Guman the yard and the Nittany Lions the touchdown and national title. Krauss was knocked cold on the play, which was named one of college football's ten most important plays. While Tide fans got a warm memory, the play brought Krauss pain. He broke his helmet on the play, and suffered a pinched nerve. The victory assured Bryant of his fifth national title. Krauss was named the SEC Lineman of the Year for 1976, an All-America in 1977–78 and was the first defensive player to be named the MVP of the Sugar Bowl, in 1978.

Krauss was the sixth player taken overall in the 1979 NFL draft, by the Baltimore Colts, and remained with the team through the move to Indianapolis and on through the 1988 season. He made more than a thousand tackles wearing a Colts uniform and received the Ed Block Courage Award.

His childhood wish came true in 1989, when he joined the Dolphins, then coached by Don Shula. He was named their captain and led the team in tackles, and at the end of the season was named the MVP. He also received a special letter that year—from his third-grade teacher. "See," she wrote him, "dreams do come true." Krauss played through 1991.

Unlike many ballplayers who move into the coaching ranks, Krauss became a businessman, then a broadcaster and motivational speaker. Krauss and Tide teammate Joe Moore collaborated on a book released in August 2006 called *Ain't Nothing But a Winner: Bear Bryant, the Goal Line Stand and a Chance of a Lifetime.*

Following pages: Tucker Frederickson (20) breaks through the line for Auburn University. *Auburn University Sports Information Office.*

20

12

He continues to broadcast Indiana Firebirds Arena League games and finally took the plunge into coaching. In 2002, he became president and head coach of the Indiana Tornadoes, a minor league professional team in the National American Football League. In their first season the Tornadoes went 13–2.

Bill Dimitrouleas was a multi-sport athlete for the Golden Tornadoes, but is probably remembered best as a champion weights specialist, especially in the discus. Dimitrouleas went on to Furman, where he continued to participate in track and field. He was named to the school's athletic hall of fame in 1999. He went on to the University of Florida Law School. He served two years in the Broward public defenders office, twelve in the state attorney's office, then donned a judge's robes, first for nine years as a circuit court judge, then starting in 1998, as a U.S. district court judge. He continues to compete in the discus and shot put in master's competition.

For *Don E. Beattie Jr.*, see Golf, and *Pam Kruse*, see Swimming.

SOUTH BROWARD HIGH SCHOOL

South Broward High School was established in 1949. The teams are nicknamed the Bulldogs.

Ivan Charles "Tucker" Frederickson excelled on the football field as well as the track for the Bulldogs. He won the state Class 2A shot put title in 1961, with a toss of 55 feet 9¾ inches, but it was on the football field where he was at his best. After South Broward, Frederickson went onto Auburn University, then to the New York Giants, where he played from 1965 to 1971, but injuries limited his accomplishments. The father of three now lives with his second wife in northern Palm Beach County. His wife, Stella, is the daughter of golfer Gardner Dickinson.

Travis Daniels, a first team all-state football player for the Bulldogs, who went on to Louisiana State University, then became the first player drafted by the Miami Dolphins since Piper's Bobby Harden in 1990. Daniels, who was drafted by the Dolphins in 2005, and immediately became a valued contributor to the team, attributes his catlike reflexes and athletic prowess to dance lessons he took as a youth.

Danny McManus played quarterback at FSU, then a year for the Kansas City Chiefs and went on to play for the Winnipeg Bombers of the Canadian Football League.

Defensive tackle *Bill Hawkins* went on to star at the University of Miami, but injuries cut short his first year with the Los Angeles Rams.

St. Thomas Aquinas High School

St. Thomas Aquinas High School got its start in 1936 when St. Anthony School, which had opened in 1926, expanded to add high school grades. In 1952 the upper grades were taken from St. Anthony's and reopened as Central Catholic High, then later given its present name. Aquinas teams are nicknamed the Raiders. In 2005 *Sports Illustrated* named the St. Thomas Aquinas athletic program the third-best in the nation.

Perhaps the greatest single success story to come from Aquinas is that of *Dr. Stefan Humphries*, who played in the NFL for the Bears and Broncos before attending medical school.

At St. Thomas, he was a standout athlete in football, where he was named All-America, as well as in basketball and track and field. He was equally impressive in the classroom, graduating as valedictorian. He went on to the University of Michigan, where he graduated magna cum laude with a 3.77 GPA in bioengineering and was a three-time NCAA Academic All-America, two-time all–Big Ten and a first-team NCAA All-America in his senior year. In 1984 he was named the Big Ten Athlete of the Year.

Humphries was selected in the third round (seventy-first overall) of 1984 draft by the Chicago Bears, where he played until 1986 in the team's Super Bowl XX championship season, defeating the New England Patriots, 46–10. In 1987–88 he went on to play for the Denver Broncos and was part of Denver's Super Bowl XXII team that lost to the Washington Redskins.

After a torn tendon in his right arm sidelined him in 1989, Humphries decided to retire from the NFL and enrolled in the University of Colorado School of Medicine. His studies were aided with the award of an NCAA postgraduate scholarship. He chose the field of rehabilitative medicine and works largely with stroke and multiple sclerosis victims.

The school was Central Catholic High when running back *Brian Piccolo* played there. As a member of the class of 1961, Piccolo lettered in several sports, but excelled in football. He went on to Wake Forest, where he led the nation his senior year, with 1,044 yards and 111 points, and finished tenth in voting for the 1964 Heisman Trophy. The word "piccolo" means "small" in Italian and Piccolo's small stature, not his determination or ability, is what kept him out of the NFL draft. He signed as a free agent with the Chicago Bears, and during his tenure with the team rushed 258 times for 927 yards and four touchdowns. He also caught 58 passes for 537 yards and another touchdown.

Brian Piccolo during his days at Wake Forest. *Wake Forest University Athletic Department.*

During the 1969 season, Piccolo found himself feeling ill and had tests done, revealing embryonal cell carcinoma, a rare and aggressive form of cancer. In the sixties and early seventies, that type of cancer was considered virtually incurable. By the twenty-first century, it can now be overcome. Despite several surgeries and other therapies, Piccolo died eight months later, on June 16, 1970. His friendship with teammate Gale Sayers and his battle against cancer were chronicled in the book and film *Brian's Song*.

The Bears retired his number 41 jersey, and since 1970, the Chicago rookie who best epitomizes the qualities Piccolo demonstrated—humor, fierce determination, loyalty and courage—has been presented the Brian Piccolo Award. In 1992 the award was changed to also recognize a veteran demonstrating those same attributes. Back in Broward, St. Thomas Aquinas named its football stadium in his honor, and a county park in Cooper City was named for him as well.

A dazzling wide receiver with breathtaking speed and elusiveness, *Michael Irvin* played for the Raiders from 1980 to 1984 then headed off to the University of Miami, where he played a big role in the Hurricanes' 1987 national title season. He left Miami early, as a junior, after amassing 2,480 yards and 27 touchdowns off 147 receptions—all team records. The Dallas Cowboys made him the eleventh overall pick in the 1988 NFL draft and Irvin played an important role in three Super Bowl years. In 1992 he was named MVP of the Pro Bowl. A neck injury in a 13–10 loss to the Philadelphia Eagles in 1999 temporarily paralyzed him and proved to be the last injury of his career. He retired at thirty-one in July 2000 and became a football commentator.

On the eve of the 2007 Super Bowl in Miami, Irvin learned he was one of six former players named to the Pro Football Hall of Fame, bringing full circle a career that had begun about forty years before in a three-bedroom house in northwestern Fort Lauderdale where Walter and Pearl Irvin raised their nine daughters and eight sons. With the honor, Irvin became the first Broward County native selected for the Pro Football Hall of Fame.

Richie Andrews got the opportunity to kick in the Blockbuster, Sugar and two Fiesta Bowls during his years at Florida State University—1987 through 1990. He and Raiders teammate Slip Watkins were drafted by the Lions in the 1991 draft. Andrews was picked in the sixth round, with the 151st pick.

Cameron Benson was named an all-state wide receiver three times while playing for the Raiders. He went on to Illinois, where he lettered for three years, hauling in 28 passes for 340 yards and a touchdown. He played in the Liberty and Rose bowls and signed as a free agent with the Tampa Bay Bucs in 1984.

In 1981 *John Congemi* quarterbacked the Raiders to their first undefeated season in school history. After graduating from St. Thomas, Congemi attended the University of Pittsburgh, where he established a school single-game record for passing (since broken), throwing for 446 yards and 5 touchdowns in one game, and throwing a 75-yard touchdown pass to Craig Heyward against Syracuse in 1986. He went on to play in the Canadian Football League for the Toronto Argonauts, Ottawa Rough Riders and Baltimore Stallions.

Sterling Palmer gained first-hand experience of one of the more interesting—and bizarre—professional football leagues in history, the made-for-TV

Daryl Porter checks over the opposing defense at Boston College. *Boston College Athletic Department.*

XFL, created in a partnership of pro wrestling's Vince McMahon and NBC. Palmer was drafted in the 17th round—140th overall—of the 2000 XFL draft by the Las Vegas Outlaws, who waived him. He was then picked up by the Chicago Enforcers. The Orlando Rage acquired him for a 2001 draft pick, but the XFL never made it to a second season. Palmer also was drafted by the NFL out of Florida State, where he played defensive end and was named the Seminoles' most dominating player in 1983. Palmer was drafted in the fourth round of the Washington Redskins in the 1993 NFL draft, where he played 49 games, posting 10 sacks. After a two-year hiatus, he went to the Patriots and later returned to the Redskins.

Daryl Porter went from St. Thomas to Boston College then on to a six-year career in the NFL, with stops at Detroit, three years in Buffalo and a year each with Tennessee and New England. Porter now owns and operates a sports bar and grill (Porter's Place) in Sunrise.

Twan Russell took the trip down to Miami for college ball, where he played linebacker and was a standout on special teams. After his years there, he was taken by the Washington Redskins in the 1997 draft and also played for the Atlanta Falcons and near home with the Miami Dolphins. Injuries forced him from the game in 2004. Russell now works in the Dolphins' front office and runs a reading foundation for children.

Diminutive running back *Tony Sands* carried the ball fifty-eight times against Missouri to earn Kansas University's game rushing record of 396 yards, then his teammates and the fans carried him off the field. He ran for 1,442 yards that season, both NCAA records at the time.

It seems everyone knows *Walker Lee Watkins* by the nickname he earned as a child—Slip. By the time he got to St. Thomas, his talent as a football player and sprinter was evident. After starring as a halfback for the Raiders' football team as well as on the track, he went on to Louisiana State to play football and run track, but he was moved to split end and wide receiver to take greater advantage of his speed. He was drafted by the Detroit Lions in the 1991 NFL draft as a kick returner, but it was as a sprinter where he achieved most acclaim.

Sanya Richards, a Jamaica-born quarter miler, went from St. Thomas to the University of Texas, was named USA Track and Field's 2006 Jesse Owens Award winner, symbolizing America's top track and field athlete.

Her years at St. Thomas Aquinas had a profound effect on her, she said. "I really enjoyed going to STA," she said. "I think I really valued the experience more once I reached college." Richards won a gold medal in the 2004 Athens Olympics for running the third leg on the United States' four-by-four-hundred-meter relay.

Seilala and *Claire Sua*, daughters of former Brigham Young University defensive tackle Mua Sua, went on to distinguish themselves in several sports. Seilala was a standout in softball, but was best as a weights specialist in track and field. She went on to UCLA as America's top prep thrower, and got better and better in college, where she was a six-time All-America performer. She went on to represent the United States in the

Tony Sands ran over, under and around defenses at St. Thomas, then also did so at Kansas. *Broward County Historical Commission, Sun-Tattler collection. Photo by Mike Stocker.*

discus in the Sydney and Athens Olympics. Claire Sua enjoyed volleyball and softball at St. Thomas and went on to UCLA to play softball, where she became a first team All-America as a designated player. Both Suas remain in California as coaches. Seilala is an assistant track coach at Cal State Northridge; Claire is an assistant softball coach at Cal Poly.

Mike Stanley was a standout baseball and football player for the Raiders, earning all-state honors in both sports. But when the time came to make a choice, baseball won his heart. In 1981 he led the county in hitting, with a .537 batting average. He went on to start all four years at the University

of Florida, where he was all-SEC. He was drafted by the Texas Rangers in 1985 and played catcher, first base and designated for the Yankees, Red Sox, Blue Jays and Athletics. He was an American League all-star in 1994. He played fifteen seasons in the Major Leagues, retiring at thirty-seven, amassing 187 home runs and a lifetime batting average of .271 in his 1,467 games. In 2005 Stanley, along with former Colorado Rockies player Dante Bichette, served as coaches for the Maitland (Florida) Little League All-Stars, who went on to reach the quarterfinals of the Little League World Series. Stanley's son Tanner played first base for the team.

For Bradley Ally, *Vladislav Polyakov* and *Paige Zemina* see Swimming. For *Julia Boros-Petit*, see Golf. For *Lisa "Lele" Forood* and *Chris*, *Claire*, *Drew* and *Jeanne Evert*, see Tennis.

Slip Watkins heads toward a touchdown for St. Thomas Aquinas. *Broward County Historical Commission, Sun-Tattler collection.*

SOUTH PLANTATION HIGH SCHOOL

South Plantation High's teams are nicknamed the Paladins, and like Furman University's Paladins, wear purple and gold.

Alfredo Roberts was named second team all-state in football and baseball (at catcher and second base) for the Paladins, but chose to go on to play football at the University of Miami. During his tenure at UM, he played tight end on two national champion teams. He was drafted in the eighth round of the 1988 NFL draft by the Kansas City Chiefs, where he played for three years. He went to the Dallas Cowboys in 1991 as a free agent and played on Dallas's 1991 and 1992 Super Bowl championship teams. Although Roberts was better known for his blocking, he made 48 receptions for 450 yards and two touchdowns as a pro.

After his playing career ended, he became a part owner of the Cowboy Café in Dallas, but when his old college coach, Howard Schnellenberger, asked him to serve as tight end and offensive line coach for his new program at Florida Atlantic University, Roberts headed back to Florida. He served at FAU for two years, then joined the staff of the Jacksonville Jaguars in 2003.

Stranahan High School

Named for Fort Lauderdale city father Frank Stranahan, Stranahan High School opened in 1953. Its teams are nicknamed the Dragons.

Rubin Carter was the heavy favorite for the Dragons in every athletic endeavor he competed in. He was a top performer on the football field and a weights specialist on the track and field team. In the latter, he held the state scholastic shot put title for fifteen years. His throw of sixty-two feet, one inch won the state Class C title in 1971. He was Broward County's Athlete of the Year in 1971 and named to the Broward County Sports Hall of Fame in 1981 and the Florida Track and Field Hall of Fame in 1999. At the University of Miami, Carter placed his emphasis on football and became one of the most dominating defensive tackles in the nation, setting a Hurricanes single-season record for tackles by a defensive tackle with ninety-eight in 1973. He was named the MVP of the 1975 Hula Bowl and to Kodak, Associated Press and United Press International All-America in 1974. He was inducted into the Hurricanes' Sports Hall of Fame in 1992.

The Denver Broncos picked him in the fifth round of the 1974 draft. He played twelve seasons as nose tackle in the famed "Orange Crush" defense, including three Super Bowls. He retired in 1986, the same year he was presented the NFL's Ed Block Award of Courage.

His coaching career has included professional and collegiate stops. On the professional level, he served as defensive line/strength and conditioning coach with the Broncos from 1987 to 1988. From 1999 to 2000 he worked as defensive line coach with the Washington Redskins and in 2001–03 coached the New York Jets defensive line. His college coaching career included stops at an assistant at Howard, San Jose State, Maryland and Temple. In July 2005 he was named Florida A&M's head football coach.

Reynaldo Hill was an all-county and all-region defensive back and cornerback while at Stranahan, then played football and ran track at Dodge City Community College. His final collegiate stop was at Florida before being drafted by the Tennessee Titans in the seventh round of the 2005 NFL draft.

Running back *Mark Rush* played for the University of Miami in 1979–82, where he roomed with quarterback Jim Kelly. He also was Kelly's teammate with the Houston Gamblers of the United States Football League. Rush was drafted one hundredth in the fourth round of the 1983 NFL draft, by the Minnesota Vikings. Another running back, *Russ Smith*, also played for the University of Miami, then was drafted by the San Diego Chargers, then of the American Football League. He played four years with the Chargers (1967–70), including their first year in the NFL. He married and became father to a daughter, Amber Smith, now a fashion model and actress.

Skip Smith is an athlete of a different sort. He has found his niche in the water, but not as a swimmer, diver or water polo player. Smith held more than forty-five International Game Fish Association records and

Brandon Kiick—whose grandfather, George, played football for the Pittsburgh Steelers, and whose father, Jim, played for the undefeated Miami Dolphins 1972 team—played football himself at Stranahan High. Jim Kiick, who also played for the Redskins, Broncos and the Memphis Southmen of the short-lived World Football League, still lives in South Florida and runs a sports promotions company in Fort Lauderdale. This picture shows Brandon and Jim Kiick. *Broward County Historical Commission, Sun-Tattler collection. Photo by Jim Urick.*

is recognized as one of the world's most influential sports fishermen of all time.

Baseball player *John Hope*, a right-handed pitcher, played from 1993 to 1996 for the Pittsburgh Pirates.

For *Miljce Donev*, see Soccer.

J.P. Taravella High School

Established in 1980 and named for one of Coral Springs's city fathers, Joseph P. Taravella, the school's teams are nicknamed the Trojans.

As he prepared for his senior year with the Trojans, *Dan Morgan* faced a dilemma: would he be the offensive or defensive workhorse for his team? He chose defense, and although he still played a bit at fullback, and had rushed for 1,332 yards and 13 touchdowns as a junior, but he also was a mainstay as linebacker. He went on to the University of Miami, where he became the nation's preeminent linebacker. He became the first player to win college's big three defensive awards—The Butkus, Bednarik and Nagurski awards. Morgan was drafted by the Carolina Panthers, where he has played since 2001. His all-out aggressive play has resulted in several concussions.

Todd Weiner, a two-time all-county football selection, Weiner also was named MVP his senior year with the Trojans, where he played tight end and guard on offense and tackle and end on defense. He went on to play at Kansas State, where he was a consensus all–Big 12 player and a second team All-America in 1997. He was then drafted in the second round of the 1998 draft (forty-seventh overall), by the Seattle Seahawks. He played for Seattle through 2001, then was signed as an unrestricted free agent a few months before the start of spring training in 2002.

Western High School

Western High School is located in the city of Davie. Its teams are nicknamed the Wildcats.

For *David Winner*, see the Soccer section in the Sports of All Sorts chapter.

WESTMINSTER ACADEMY

Westminster Academy was established in 1971. Its teams are nicknamed the Lions.

Danny Kanell set records in baseball and football. In his senior year on the Lions football team, he threw for 1,528 yards and 18 touchdowns, and was considered one of the top prep quarterbacks in the nation.

Kanell chose Florida State, which allowed him to play football and baseball. In football, he earned first team All-America honors and threw for 6,372 yards and 57 touchdowns. He leads the Seminoles quarterbacks with ten 300-yard passing games. His single-best effort was 454 yards against Virginia in 1995.

Kanell was chosen by the New York Giants in the fourth round of the 1996 draft, the 130th overall selection. He spent three years in New York, including leading the Giants to the playoffs in his second season there. He also played two years with the Atlanta Falcons, and then after a long hiatus to repair and rehabilitate a knee injury, he completed his NFL career in Denver. During the hiatus, he spent a year playing for the New York Dragons in the Arena Football League. During his NFL years, he completed 491 of 956 attempts for 5,129 yards.

For *Dana Kanell*, see Tennis.

9

Colleges

Two postsecondary educational institutions currently make their home in Broward County: Broward Community College and Nova Southeastern University (NSU). Both offer extensive athletic programs.

Broward Community College (BCC) started its athletic program in 1962, two years after the college opened its doors. The men's basketball team, under the direction of Hubert Wright, played its games at Stranahan High School in Fort Lauderdale. The golf team played at Orangebrook Golf Course in Hollywood and the baseball team, coached by Eddie Harris, practiced at New River Middle School but played its games at Holiday Park in Fort Lauderdale.

Tennis was the first women's sports program offered, starting in 1964, under the guidance of physical education professor Elaine Gavigan. The tennis program has gone on to become the college's most successful team, winning four National Junior College Athletic Association (NJCAA) championships, starting with the first in 1996 under head coach Tom Burke. The team added a pair of national titles in 2003 and 2004 under Patrick Catullo and again in 2006 under LeTrone Mason. Wendy Fine was the first BCC tennis player to be named to an All-America team, in 1980. Since then more than fifty players have won designation as All-America, including Jackie Castillejo (1983), Nina Schmidt (1988), Teresa Stromberg (1993), Edith Tieber (1996), Adolfina Hadamovsky (1996), Vesna McKenna (1996), Marine Nizri (1997–98), Radka Sottova (2003), Leigh Shelton (2004), Karine Ionesco (2004), Marta Simic (2006), Chandra Capozzi (2006), Adrienne Duenas (2006), Romy Farah (2006) and Monica Ortega (2006).

Above: Coach Tom Burke led Broward Community College's women's tennis team to its first national title in 1996. *Broward Community College.*

Opposite: Nina Schmidt, Steffi Graf's childhood friend, was Broward Community College's second NJCAA individual national champion and an NJCAA All-America in 1987 and 1988. *Broward Community College.*

Following pages: R.L. Landers with one of BCC's women's golf teams. *Broward Community College*.

Originally, BCC's sports mascot was the Seahorse. Central Campus, located in Davie, was the home of the college's athletic program until the early 1970s, when the North Campus opened in Coconut Creek. The college responded to its growth spurt by fielding teams from North and Central Campuses. North Campus fielded a basketball team in 1972, and women's sports were added about that time as well. The Central Campus teams remained the Seahorses and the North Campus program operated as the Trotters, in recognition of nearby Pompano Park harness track. Multiple teams caused a fiscal drain on the student affairs budget and the college in 1986–87 decided to offer a unified program with some teams housed at North Campus, some at Central. The program was unified under a new mascot, the Seahawks.

The program benefited from savvy administrators, such as Rex Brumley, R.L. Landers and Alton "Andy" Andrews, who guided it during the college's early years, and BCC athletes have always benefited from outstanding coaching. Among the most memorable have been Leroy Wheat, a former Philadelphia Athletics pitcher, who led the baseball program through its formative years; Hal Blitman, who had coached the Miami Floridians of the American Basketball Association and the men's basketball team, and All-America softball player Judy Blucker, who coached volleyball, softball and women's basketball. Bud Marsee, who coached the men's golf team to a pair of NJCAA national championships, went on to become the first coach of Auburn University's women's golf team. The BCC women's golf team also fared well, winning the NJCAA national championship in 1980.

The 1974 men's national championship team was the steppingstone for two young men who made a significant impact in the world of golf. Mike Donald, a Nova High graduate, went on to Georgia Southern University, then to the PGA Tour. He won the 1989 Anheuser-Busch Classic and tied the Masters's record for low first-round score—sixty-four—by a rookie. His teammate, Don Beattie, entered the PGA, but enjoyed the teaching and administrative aspects of the sport. Like Donald, he went on to Georgia Southern, then became an assistant pro at Pompano Beach's municipal golf course. He became director of golf at the Polo Club in Boca Raton from 1985 to 1993, then moved north to run the Medallion Club, in Columbus, Ohio, from 1993 to 1996. Beattie returned to Florida in 1996 to become director of golf at Addison Reserve, in western Delray Beach, then signed on as director of golf at Mirasol, in Palm Beach Gardens, from the club's opening in 2001 until his sudden death in June 2006.

Janis Drummonds, who went on to a career as a coach, was an outstanding basketball player for BCC. *Broward County Historical Commission, Sun-Tattler collection.*

As of 2006, Broward Community College's Athletic Hall of Fame has eighteen members. They are athletic administrator Rex Brumley, tennis coach Tom Burke, volleyball coach Louise Crocco, basketball player Janis Drummonds, tennis player Wendy Fine, swimmer Montsi Gomariz, volleyball player Holly Greene, diver Dawn Trainor Holmquist, swimmer Mike Lane, golf coach Bud Marsee, basketball coach Clinton Morris, athletic administrator Tom Ryan, basketball player Greg Samuel, tennis player Nina Schmidt, baseball player Craig Skok, swimmer Seth Van Neerden, baseball coach Lee Wheat and vice-president for student affairs Dr. George Young.

In 1980 Dr. Abraham Fischler, president of Nova University, authorized the start of an athletic program as a means of stimulating undergraduate enrollment. Most of Nova's early enrollment was on the graduate level, particularly educators who took advantage of the university's satellite programs offered on nights and weekends at locations around the nation.

Sonny Hansley was named the school's first athletic director and head basketball coach in 1981, and the next year the team's nickname—Knights—was chosen after a name-the-team contest.

The men's basketball program started play in 1982, playing a non-conference schedule, then the university's program grew steadily, adding men's and women's teams.

Dag Cohen, a freshman midfielder, from Borgholm, Sweden, was the first Nova player named to an All-America team, selected to the National Soccer Coaches Association team in 1986.

Nova University merged with North Miami Beach-based Southeastern University of the Health Sciences in 1994, changing its name to Nova Southeastern University. In 2002 the university became a member of NCAA Division II. Kyle Ruwe, a pitcher on the Knights baseball team, was the university's first NCAA All-America player, named to the second team in 2003. In 2004 sixth-seat rower Jennifer Rembe became the university's first female All-America athlete, selected to the Collegiate Rowing Coaches Association's first team.

Teofilo "Coquito" Cubillas Jr. son of the Fort Lauderdale Strikers midfielder, became the first NSU player drafted by Major League Soccer, when he was selected in the 2001 MLS Super Draft.

Nova and another member of the Sunshine State Conference, Lynn University of Boca Raton, claimed the Knights as their mascot, so in 2005, Nova changed its nickname to Sharks. The name was determined as the first had been—with a name-the-team contest.

Currently NSU offers eight varsity sports for women and five for men. In 2006, in recognition of the university's twenty-fifth year of athletics, Nova announced the formation of the NSU Athletic Hall of Fame. Members of the first class were announced in January 2007. They are soccer player Teofilo Cubillas Jr., President Emeritus Abraham Fischler, first athletic director and former men's basketball and baseball coach Sonny Hansley, basketball player David Riley and softball player Shannon Sawyer.

Bibliography

Amdur, Neil. "An American Original." *World Tennis*, December 1989.

Archer, Todd. "Third time's a charm for Michael Irvin." *(San Jose) Mercury News*, February 3, 2007.

Barnes, Craig. "Irvin so happy he could bust." *South Florida Sun-Sentinel*, February 4, 2007.

———. "McClover's heart stays with prep coach." *South Florida Sun-Sentinel*, January 31, 2007.

Berrios, Jerry and Nirvi Shah. "Stadium redo for O's gets a lift." *Miami Herald*, September 28, 2006.

Board, Prudy Taylor. *The History of Dania Beach: A Century of Pioneer Spirit*. Virginia Beach, VA: The Donning Company, 2004.

Bricker, Charles. "Blake, Merklein have come full circle." *South Florida Sun-Sentinel*, November 28, 2006.

———. "Jags' Gray plays waiting game." *South Florida Sun-Sentinel*. November 29, 2006.

Cahill, William P. "The First Sheriffs of Broward County, Florida: 1915–1933." *Broward Legacy* 24:3, 2003–2004.

Cavaioli, Frank J. *Images of America: Pompano Beach*. Charleston, SC: Arcadia Publishing, 2003.

Cosco, Joseph. "The drags." *Fort Lauderdale News and Sun-Sentinel*, December 21, 1980.

Cuddy, Don. *Tales of Old Hollywood*. Decatur, IL: Spectator Books, 1977.

Finder, Chuck. "Blades cuts a different family legacy." *Pittsburgh Post-Gazette*, November 29, 2003 (online edition).

Flink, Steve. "The Way She Was," *World Tennis*, December 1989.

Gillis, Susan. *Fort Lauderdale: The Venice of America*. Charleston, SC: Arcadia Publishing, 1999.

Goodman, Joseph. "Ely names football coach," *Miami Herald*, February 2, 2007.

Hamilton, Katie Phipps. Letter to Broward County Historical Commission. BCHC files.

Howard, Johnette. "The Rivals: Chris Evert vs. Martina Navratilova: Their Epic Duels and Extraordinary Friendship." New York: Broadway Books, 2005.

Jacobs, Sonji. "Historic Plunge." *Miami Herald*, September 3, 2002.

Kaiser, Dave. "First Family of Tennis." *Set Point*, September–October 1973.

Kluepfel, Brian. "Mark Chung: American Soccer's Coolest Man." *Asian Week* (online edition), November 29–December 5, 2002.

Markowitz, Dan. "No longer child's play." *Tennis Week*, July 20, 2006.

Marra, Andrew and Thom Smith. "Evert, Mill to divorce." *Palm Beach Post*, October 21, 2006.

Martin, G. Harold. Letter to Broward County Historical Commission, January 7, 1993.

Martin, Harold. "Real baseball provided by the East Coast League." *Miami Herald*, May 9, 1925.

Martin, Scott. "Bushwood No More." *Florida Golf Journal*, Fall 2006.

Marvez, Alex. "A first for FIU: Former DB set to play for Falcons." *South Florida Sun-Sentinel*, November 12, 2006.

McCormack, John. "Former world champion took title, life in stride." *Miami Herald*, April 4, 1982.

McGoun, Bill. *Hallandale*. Hallandale, FL.: Hallandale Historical Society, 1976.

McIver, Stuart. *The Island City: The Story of Wilton Manors*. Wilton Manors, FL: City of Wilton Manors, 1997.

Mell, Randall. "New look for Inverrary." *South Florida Sun-Sentinel*, December 31, 2006.

Mickelson, Joan. *A Guide to Historic Hollywood*. Charleston, SC: The History Press, 2005.

Patterson, Paige. "Hollywood lobs pitch for Expos." *Hollywood Sun*, April 4, 1991.

Persall, Steve. "Off the field, Mark Zupan still carries the ball." *St. Petersburg Times* (online edition), July 28, 2005.

Plaschke, Bill. "…But cold fails to keep her from swimming record." *Fort Lauderdale News*, December 10, 1981.

Povtak, Tim. "Little League champs get big-league help." *Orlando Sentinel*, August 6, 2005.

Robb, Sharon. "Richards takes honors." *South Florida Sun-Sentinel*, November 29, 2006.

Robert, C. Richard. *Images of America: Hollywood*. Charleston, SC: Arcadia Publishing, 2002.

Shine, T.M. "What a drag!" *Sun-Sentinel*. December 9, 1992.

Simms, Louis M. *In Place of Pearls*. Hamilton, New Zealand: Rimu Press, 1984.

Soler, Eileen. "How the West was fun." *Miami Herald*, September 11, 2004.

Sullivan, Russell. *Rocky Marciano: The Rock of His Times*. Urbana: University of Illinois Press, 2002.

Sympson, Ron. "To diDonatos today marks 'the ultimate.'" *Fort Lauderdale News and Sun-Sentinel*, August 9, 1981.

"Tee me off, suckers: How do you erase a golf course?" *New Times*, November 2–8, 2006.

TenEick, Virginia Elliott. *History of Hollywood (1920 to 1950)*. Miami: McMurray Printers, 1966.

Weidling, Philip and August Burghard. *Checkered Sunshine: The History of Fort Lauderdale, 1793–1955*. Fort Lauderdale, FL: Wake-Brook House/Fort Lauderdale Historical Society, 1974.

Wieczorek, Dave. "Stella: She's back in the splash and not just for the fun." *Fort Lauderdale News*, April 1, 1981.

Zupan, Mark. *Gimp*. New York: HarperCollins Publishers, 2006.